Celebrate the Jewish Holidays
with RACHELI MORRIS

This must-have book for the lady of the house
is full of unique ideas to welcome and delight your
guests and enrich your holiday celebration.

• More than 70 table settings inspired by the traditions of the
Jewish holidays • Fascinating information on the history and
significance of the Jewish holidays • More than 50 delicious recipes
• Creative cupcake ideas for each holiday
• Ideas to involve your children with creative projects that will
help them appreciate and follow Jewish traditions

Author: Racheli Morris

Editor: Roxanne Tretheway

Editorial consultants:
Suzette Lavine, Noah Hurvitz, Cherille Berman, Joni Prinjinski

Photography: Racheli Morris

Food Styling: Racheli Morris

Table Designs: Racheli Morris

Graphic Design: Dorothy Wineman
& Racheli Morris

ISBN 978-0-578-16018-4

Library of Congress Cataloging-in-Publication Date

Printed in USA

All Scripture quotations are taken with permission from
http://www.mechon-mamre.org

Visit our website at www.rachelimorris.com

author@rachelimorris.com

Telephone (949) 309-0322

This book is dedicated to my mother, Malka Arbiv, and to the memory of my late father, Nathan Arbiv, who have always given me love and believed in me; for this I owe them a great debt of gratitude.

Recognition

A beautiful Jewish tradition is to begin correspondence with "BH," reminding us that all things come from God. The BH can stand for *Baruch HaShem* (blessed be God) or *B'ezrat HaShem* (God's help). With this idea in mind, I wish to recognize those whom God provided to help me bring this book to publication.

First and foremost, of course, I would like to thank God, the father of Abraham, Isaac and Jacob. It is He who gave me the motivation and strength to work through this beautiful book from beginning to end. May He be honored in these pages.

To Brian Morris and our dear lovely children, Jonathan and Jennifer, the lights of my life and the reason for my happiness. Thank you for all of the patience, encouragement and good humor you provided throughout the project.

To my siblings and extended family who believed in me all along.

To Roger Kershaw, I did not believe in miracles until I met you! Thank you for the invaluable support you gave to me throughout the entire project, for mentoring me in a professional manner, and for giving me your full trust.

To Roxanne Tretheway, the editor of this book. You are a woman who meets every challenge with a positive spirit, you always provided constructive advice and it was a great privilege to work with you.

To Dorothy Wineman, a graphic artist who works intelligently, methodically and transfers her creativity onto every page.

I would like to thank the directors and staff of Hebrew at the Center, especially President Arnee Winshall, Director and Professor Vardit Ringvald and Frieda Robins, school advisor, who generously provided indispensable mentorship, not only professionally, but spiritually and personally; they have taught and inspired me to become a leader in the Jewish community.

To the Tenenbaum family, the great leaders of Chabad of Irvine, who were consistently kind and encouraging.

To the members and management team of Temple Beth El for allowing me the great privilege of creating stunning table settings in the synagogue.

To Mody Gorsky, publisher of *Orange County Jewish Life Magazine*, thank you for giving me the opportunity to write articles on Jewish hospitality, the spark that ignited the idea for this book.

To Shahrokh and Julie Ghodsi, owners of the Judaica store The Golden Dreidle, for the cheerful encouragement you gave so freely.

To my talented and good friends Noah Hurvitz, Cherille Berman, Suzette Lavine, Lidia Blum, Joni Prinjinski, and Sigal Konchitski. Each of these remarkable friends spent long hours providing assistance and advice throughout the creative process.

A big thank you to Dove Canyon Country Club and the outstanding and wonderful women of Orange County who were great listeners and allowed me to spend hours and hours in their beautiful homes in order to set the unique table settings found in these pages.

Celebrate the
Jewish Holidays
WITH RACHELI MORRIS

This book is the premiere guide for elegant and stylish Jewish hospitality. In it, I share my secrets for having fun while entertaining guests in a sophisticated, creative and festive manner. You'll discover your own creative side as you set your table for the holidays. Whether it's a warm Shabbat dinner or a stunning Rosh HaShanah feast, your guests will be amazed and delighted!

Entertaining is more than a multicourse meal. It is about gathering family and friends together and making memories. This book will help you put all the details together so that your event will be stunning, meaningful and joyful.

From my table to yours,

Racheli Morris

Recipes

This book includes more than 50 traditional recipes, as well as some modern innovations on dishes for each occasion. Recipes for dishes we ate at our mothers' homes will bring treasured memories to mind. You will be delighted to find that in a very short time you can create beautiful presentations that make the occasion exceptional.

Cupcakes

Cupcakes are always a delightful addition to any holiday. Create your own specially designed cupcakes, or order unique designs from specialty shops that offer customization.

Activities

Enjoy creative pre-holiday activities with your family, setting the mood for a grand time at your holiday party. For example, for your Chanukah dinner party you can help your children bake sugar cookies in the shape of menorahs and dreidels to be put into gift boxes for your guests. Before your Yom Kippur dinner party, children can design kippot for each male guest and prepare refreshing scented apples to be used by those fasting.

Traditions

Inside the pages of this book are answers to many questions about customs and mitzvot (meritorious deeds) in the Jewish tradition. Some of these explanations are key to the rituals of Jewish holidays. For example, why do we put two challah on the table? Why do we light two candles on a Friday evening? What symbolic items do we put on the table for a Rosh HaShanah dinner and what is the significance of each?

Table Settings

You will learn simple ways to decorate your table using unique flower arrangements, as well as how to choose the right vases, dishes, and perfect colors to accentuate a beautiful table. You will also find useful and practical information about etiquette and table settings, and much, much more!

The examples given in this book are provided to inspire and excite you, to give you an opportunity to combine these ideas with your own creativity and, most of all, to have fun. Just remember, whether you are hosting a party, celebrating a holiday, or sitting down to dinner with family and friends, good food served on an elegant and beautiful table brings a sense of harmony, and makes a meal remarkable and memorable. Enjoy!

TABLE OF CONTENTS

Shabbat

Remember the sabbath day,
to keep it holy.

—EXODUS 20:7

Shabbat

Come my Beloved to greet the Bride—The Sabbath presence, let us welcome!

On Friday night, we welcome and bring in Shabbat. Shabbat comes from the Hebrew word *shavat*, to sit and rest. Shabbat is referred to as the "bride" throughout the liturgy. *L'Cha Dodi,* a traditional Shabbat song, includes a verse that welcomes Shabbat as the *kallah,* which is the Hebrew word for bride. Unlike the daily routine where everyone seems to grab their meals whenever and wherever they can, Shabbat is an occasion for the whole family to gather around the dinner table. It allows all family members to listen and be heard, to enjoy a traditional meal and to sing Shabbat songs together. This atmosphere requires an inviting table that will make the surroundings feel welcoming, and the guests feel a part of the special gathering.

Gathering on Friday night for Shabbat dinner is an essential Jewish tradition, and serving challah bread and wine is practiced by Jewish families worldwide. Two of the braided challah are served, reminding us of the two portions of manna that were gathered for the Sabbath in the Book of Exodus. Wine represents joy, reminding us that Shabbat is a time to be together as a family, resting and being happy.

At the beginning of each Shabbat, candles are lit and special blessings are said over the bread and wine.

Shabbat Bride

*For in six days the LORD made
heaven and earth, the sea,
and all that in them is, and rested
on the seventh day; wherefore
the LORD blessed the sabbath day,
and hallowed it.*

—EXODUS 20:10

Traditionally, people were shomer Shabbat, which means guarding the Sabbath and keeping it holy. Instead of working, Shabbat is a chance to spend time with family and to quietly contemplate the universe and all God has provided.

Three special meals are served over Shabbat: a wonderful Friday night dinner, a Saturday morning breakfast and a light meal late on Saturday afternoon before Havdalah. Havdalah is recited at the close of Shabbat, and a beautifully braided candle is used that is then extinguished in a cup of wine to represent the start of the new week. Fragrant spices provide a pleasing aroma to help our minds to become alert.

Shabbat celebrations are countdowns, highlighting the importance of preparation. Shavuot is a 49-day countdown once a year, but Shabbat is a weekly countdown, with the emphasis on preparation increasing as Friday night approaches. The prepared host has given attention to clean linens and supplies, such as candles and décor. Closer to Friday, care is taken to set the house in order and also to have beautiful clothes ready for celebrating this special holiday which comes 52 times a year. Shopping and food preparation occur well before meal-time on Friday night, and can include ordering special items,

as well as going grocery shopping. Food that can be prepared ahead of time, such as beef stew, helps a busy host save time. The hosts want to be fresh and ready to greet their guests on Shabbat. This sense of order and harmony is part of the Shabbat atmosphere, of Shabbat rest, into which all are welcomed.

Table Description

The table for Friday night dinner is set with two covered, braided challah, a kiddush cup, two candles and white flowers. The candles are lit by one of the women of the house, because the woman is the one who unifies her household and creates peace therein. The colors of white and silver, which are used for wedding décor, are significant for welcoming the Bride, the Beloved Shabbat. These candles are housed in a special, heirloom silver box which serves as the centerpiece for this elegant and pristine setting. A white tablecloth is set with clear, silver-striped wine glasses matching the dinner plates. Miniature champaign bottles are used as place cards, with the name of the guest printed on each bottle. This table welcomes the Bride and also makes each guest feel valued and special.

Blessed are You, LORD our God, King of the universe, who has sanctified us with His commandments, and commanded us to light the Shabbat candle[s].

Shopping and food preparation occur well before mealtime on Friday night and can include special items, such as the beautiful cupcakes in this book. I designed these especially to delight and inspire you in your creative entertaining and holiday times.

Involving the Children

Shabbat is a natural time for children to get involved in preparation activities. Feel free to invite them to try their hand at making mini-challah breads. What could be more fun than adding a few chocolate chips to the dough? The bread can be braided, rolled into a log and twisted into a small turban, or rolled up like a double Torah scroll to capture Shabbat themes.

As an alternative activity, prepare cupcakes that the children can ice. Cake shops carry a variety of stencil designs for sprinkling colored sugar. Whether a wine-glass shape, a Jewish star or candle shape, the activity will spark conversation and add to the fun of celebrating Shabbat as a family.

Shabbat Beloved Bride

...and there ye shall eat before the LORD your God, and ye shall rejoice in all that ye put your hand unto, ye and your households, wherein the LORD thy God hath blessed thee.

—DEUTERONOMY 12:7

Table Description

Inspired by the shimmering gown of a bride, this elegant white tablecloth with matching chair covers brings light and desire to the Shabbat table. On top of bright gold chargers are fine blue, white and gold china. The chargers radiate the richness and excitement of the occasion. Artistically crafted gold candle holders, golden salt and pepper pomegranates, and gold-rimmed wine glasses surround the two blue and brown challahs, which rest on a golden-handled tray. A gold-topped decanter of red wine is ready to toast the bride. The table is crowned with a tall, graceful candelabra filled with cascading blue and white flowers like the bouquet of the bride.

Shabbat Shalom

*And God blessed the seventh day, and hallowed it;
because that in it He rested from all His work
which God in creating had made.*

—GENESIS 2:3

Shabbat is the biblical day of rest. It is the most important ritual in Judaism
and is the only ritual discussed in the Ten Commandments. It begins a few
minutes before the sun sets on Friday night and ends after three stars appear
in the evening sky on Saturday, which typically occurs forty minutes after
sunset. Since sunset times vary throughout the year, Jewish calendars are
published with candle lighting times; various websites can also inform you of
the time Shabbat starts on any given Friday.

All fast days, with the exception of Yom Kippur, are postponed if they fall on
Shabbat because the memorial day of God resting after creation is meant to
be a day of festive delight, not of fasting.

Everyone dresses nicely, the family gathers, the lady of the house lights the
candles, blessings are said, wine is sipped and a spirit of thankfulness prevails.

Table Description

*Welcome your guests to Shabbat with elegant colors and a classic environment.
Ruby, gold and white create a striking table setting. Attention to detail and
matching colors will highlight the beauty of Shabbat. For instance, choose a napkin
ring that matches the pretty print of the china. Uniquely folded bow napkins add
an inviting touch. Complete the table setting with a beautiful
centerpiece of pink and red roses. Sprinkle
rose petals along the table to create a natural
table runner; a burgundy bread cover adds
another rich hue. The overall setting
shows respect for the Bride, the Beloved
Sabbath. The wine glasses are set
beside the chargers, and golden
candles stand ready for the lighting
ceremony. Shabbat Shalom!*

Festival Shabbat

Every Shabbat is a chance to remember God's provision. The sharing of the challah is a celebration of plenty, all He has provided from the land. The wine celebrates joy in the provision of the fruit of the vine. Traditionally, the male head of the household prays blessings over the challah and the wine each Shabbat and every holiday, even when those holidays do not occur on the seventh day of the week.

"See that the LORD hath given you the sabbath; therefore He giveth you on the sixth day the bread of two days; abide ye every man in his place, let no man go out of his place on the seventh day." And the house of Israel called the name thereof Manna; and it was like coriander seed, white; and the taste of it was like wafers made with honey.

—EXODUS 16:29, 31

Traditionally, the two challah are placed next to two candles with a bread cloth covering the loaves until prayer time, when the beautiful loaves are revealed. When our ancestors traveled in the desert for forty years, they survived by gathering and eating the manna that miraculously fell from heaven every day for six days, with a double portion falling on Friday: one portion for that day, and another for the day of rest that followed so they would not have to gather manna on the Sabbath. The two loaves of challah that we place on our table today represent the double portion of manna, reliving the manna miracle at our Shabbat meal; and the challah cloth represents the dew that protected the manna.

Table Description

In this table setting, the challah is made colorful to add to the family's enjoyment and children's delight. A simple white tablecloth is brightened by colorful napkins that echo the colors in the tulips and in the festive challah. Crystal stemware and square white plates with place cards slipped into the folded napkins continue the clean lines of this table. Red wine in a graceful decanter reflects its rich ruby color onto the white tablecloth.

Festival Challah

(Pareve) Makes 2 challah

7 cups flour

2 teaspoons salt

1½ tablespoons instant yeast

½ cup sugar

¾ cup canola oil

2 eggs

2 cups warm water

Food coloring (three colors)

1 egg, beaten with 1 tablespoon water

Poppy or sesame seeds (optional)

Preheat oven to 375°F. Mix flour and salt together in mixing bowl. Add yeast, sugar, oil, eggs, and warm water. Mix thoroughly. Once dough has come together into a smooth ball, divide it into two portions. Cut each portion into thirds and mix each third with 4-6 drops of food coloring. Knead each colored dough on a lightly flour-covered surface and allow to rise for 40 minutes, until doubled in volume. Shape each 3-piece portion into a braided challah and allow to rise a second time for 40 minutes. Brush each braid with egg wash. If desired, sprinkle with poppy or sesame seeds. Bake 30-40 minutes, depending on the size of the challah.

Note: Food coloring can change the taste of the challah, so it's really more for fun.

Moroccan Spiced Tilapia

(Pareve) Serves 4-6

6 tilapia fillets

5 tablespoons canola oil

½ tablespoon hot paprika

1 ½ tablespoons sweet paprika

1 tablespoon turmeric

6 garlic cloves, peeled and sliced

4 tablespoons tomato paste

2 cups water

Juice of 1 lemon

1 large yellow onion, sliced into ½″ rings

1 red bell pepper, seeds removed and cut into strips

½ cup fresh cilantro, chopped

½ cup fresh parsley, chopped

1 pinch of sugar

Salt and pepper

Garnish:
1 tablespoon fresh parsley, chopped
Lemon slices

In a sauté pan, combine oil, hot and sweet paprika, turmeric and garlic. Heat for 1 minute, stirring continuously. Add tomato paste, water and lemon juice, stirring until fully incorporated. Simmer on low heat for 10 minutes to slightly reduce the sauce. Add onion, bell pepper, cilantro and parsley to sauce. Season with sugar, salt, and pepper to taste. Immediately place fillets in sauce. Be certain the sauce completely covers the fillets. Cover and poach gently for 10 minutes or until cooked through. Remove fillets from pan and place on serving platter. Top with sauce and garnish with additional parsley and lemon slices.

Golden Harvest Shabbat

God's people were commanded to rejoice over the blessings they received from Him. Some special holidays were celebrated in Jerusalem. Others, like Shabbat, were celebrated at home. The entire household joined in the meal. Today, family gatherings on Shabbat are still observed, reflecting the joy of being together. The gracious host makes everyone feel welcome in the home with pleasant surroundings, beauty and harmony. White tablecloths, cloth napkins and fresh flowers are traditional complements to Shabbat meals.

Table Description

Flower arrangements can bring color, fragrance, elegance and surprise. In this table setting, a candelabra serves as a beautiful and unexpected vase where votives embrace roses and calla lilies. The contrasting color of red roses ties together the earthy tones of bronze, muted green, and gold. Antique gold votive candleholders are accented with dangling crystals, matching the candelabra centerpiece. A Battenberg lace tablecloth anchors this elegant Shabbat table. Gold chargers echo the golden accents on the crystal stemware. White plates with a gold rim and golden leaf pattern follow the theme of the evening.

O come, let us sing unto the LORD; let us shout for joy to the Rock of our salvation.

—PSALM 95:1

23

Beef Stew

(Meat) Serves 4-6

2½ pounds stewing beef, cubed

Salt and pepper

1 tablespoon dry mustard

2 tablespoons vegetable oil

3 large potatoes, peeled
  and cut into 1″ pieces

4 large carrots, chopped

3 celery stalks, chopped

1 medium onion, chopped

6 garlic cloves, peeled and sliced

2 leeks cleaned well, sliced (only
  use white and light green parts)

4 ounces white mushrooms, roughly chopped

¼ cup tomato paste

1 cup red wine

¼ cup red wine vinegar

1 15-ounce can diced tomatoes with juice

3½ cups beef stock

1 teaspoon sea salt

2 bay leaves

1 sprig fresh thyme

1 sprig fresh rosemary

⅓ cup fresh parsley, chopped

Season beef cubes on all sides with salt, pepper and mustard. Heat oil in a 5-6 quart Dutch oven and brown beef cubes in batches over high heat, adding more oil as needed. While meat is browning, prepare vegetables. Remove beef cubes when nicely browned, leaving juices in Dutch oven. Lower heat and add vegetables (potatoes through mushrooms). Cook for 5-10 minutes until slightly softened. Stir in tomato paste and continue cooking. Return beef cubes to Dutch oven. Add wine, vinegar and tomatoes with juice. Bring to a boil. Add enough beef stock to cover ingredients. While bringing to a boil, add salt, bay leaves, thyme and rosemary. Simmer, partially covered, for 2-3 hours until meat is tender. Before serving, add half the parsley. Garnish with remaining parsley.

Eggplant with Parsley and Garlic
(Pareve) Serves 4-6

2 eggplants, sliced ¾″ thick

½ cup flour

1 tablespoon canola oil

1 tablespoon brown sugar

Juice from 1½ lemons

½ cup parsley, finely chopped

2-3 garlic cloves, peeled and minced

Salt to taste

Sprinkle flour on both sides of eggplant slices (preventing eggplant from becoming too soft). Heat oil in a pan and fry eggplant slices on each side until light golden brown. Place eggplant on paper towels to absorb excess oil. In a small bowl, mix together remaining ingredients. Arrange eggplant slices on a large platter and spread mixture over the top. Wait 20 minutes, then serve.

From the rising of the sun unto the going down
thereof the LORD's name is to be praised.

—PSALM 113:3

Celebration in Blue

When everyone arrives at the home for the Sabbath meal, the table has already been set. Before the meal is shared, the family gathers for Sabbath blessings, but first the family sings together. A popular choice is *Shalom Aleichem*. In this environment, a holy feeling fills the room. Next, the father blesses the children by placing his hand on their heads or embracing them all and reciting:

For a son: May God make you as Ephraim and Menashe
                 [the two sons of Joseph]

For a daughter: May God make you as Sarah, Rebecca, Rachel and Leah
                 [the four matriarchs of the Bible]

The father continues with the traditional blessing from the Torah, based on the Aaronic Benediction:

The LORD bless thee, and keep thee; The LORD make His face to shine upon thee, and be gracious unto thee; The LORD lift up His countenance upon thee, and give thee peace.

—NUMBERS 6:24-26

The husband then honors his wife by reading and singing this song, and all the family joins in:

A woman of valour who can find?

—PROVERBS 31:10-31

The next blessing is over the wine and is called the *Shabbat Kiddush*. Finally, the blessing over the bread, the *Motzi*, is said. After eating a small piece of bread, everyone shouts, "*Shabbat Shalom!*"

Table Description

In this table celebration, the simple white tablecloth is the background for an explosion of cobalt blue. Blue glass chargers are topped with white dinner plates and a blue-and-white patterned salad plate. Cobalt blue wine glasses and blue-handled silverware reinforce the theme. A cobalt blue charger supporting crystal candlesticks with blue candles and a blue glass vase with delicate roses makes the perfect centerpiece. Simple white napkins tied with blue ribbons complete the fresh and inviting look.

Chocolate Yeast Cake

(Pareve) Serves 6-10

Dough:

4½ cups flour

½ cup sugar

1 package of yeast

Zest of 1 lemon

⅔ cup unsalted margarine, melted

3 eggs

½ cup water, lukewarm

¼ teaspoon salt

1 egg, beaten with 1 tablespoon water

⅓ cup sesame seeds

Filling:

⅓ cup quality cocoa

1 cup confectioner's sugar

1 cup dark chocolate, melted

½ cup unsalted margarine, melted

¾ cup raisins or pecans, coarsely chopped (optional)

2 tablespoons superfine sugar

Glaze:

⅔ cup water

1¼ cups superfine sugar

Vanilla extract or rum

Pre-heat oven to 375°F. In a large bowl, mix flour, sugar, yeast, and lemon zest. Use mixer on low speed for 1 minute. Add margarine, eggs, and water. Increase to low-medium speed for 7 minutes, until dough is completely smooth and elastic. Cover dough with plastic wrap and kitchen towel. Allow dough to rise for 2 hours, until doubled in volume.

While dough is rising, prepare filling by mixing ingredients together, cocoa to margarine, or simply use a prepared chocolate spread. Set raisins/pecans and sugar to the side.

Divide dough into two portions. On a lightly flour-covered surface, roll out each portion into a 15″ x 10″ rectangle. Trim the sides to make them even. Spread filling over each rectangle, leaving a ¾″ border all around. If desired, sprinkle raisins or pecans on top of the filling, then sprinkle with sugar. Roll up rectangle, starting from the long side that is closest to you. Trim about ¾″ off both ends.

Use knife to cut roll in half lengthwise. With the cut sides facing up, gently press together the tops of each half. Gently lift the right half over the left half, and then lift the left half over the right, to create a two-pronged plait. Gently press together the bottoms of each half. Carefully place cake into a 16″ loaf pan. Cover pan with plastic wrap and kitchen towel. Allow to rise for 1 hour. Brush with egg wash and sprinkle with sesame seeds. Bake 30-40 minutes on middle rack of oven, until a cake tester comes out clean.

While cake is baking, in small saucepan boil water and sugar until the sugar dissolves. Let cool a bit, then add vanilla extract or rum to taste and mix well. When cake is done, brush glaze over the top.

Chocolate-Dipped Strawberries

(Pareve) Serves 4-6

1 pint large, long-stemmed strawberries, washed and dried

1 pound good quality dark chocolate, chopped

Whipped cream substitute

Melt chocolate in a double boiler. When fully melted, dip strawberries in the chocolate and place on wax paper to cool.

Put a small amount of remaining chocolate in a Ziploc bag and snip off a corner of the bag with scissors. When chocolate on strawberries is fully hardened, use the Ziploc bag to decorate each strawberry by drizzling the chocolate on top.

Serve with whipped cream.

Chocolate Cupcakes

(Pareve) Makes 20 cupcakes

1½ cups flour

½ teaspoon baking powder

1 teaspoon baking soda

½ cup cocoa powder

1 cup sugar

1 teaspoon salt

½ cup vegetable oil

1 tablespoon vanilla extract

1 teaspoon distilled white vinegar

1 cup water

½ cup chocolate chips

Garnish:

¾ cup dark chocolate, melted

Shredded coconut, chocolate covered sunflower seeds or other toppings

Preheat oven to 350°F. In a bowl, mix together dry ingredients.
Add remaining ingredients. Mix together well until batter is smooth.

Line muffin pan with paper inserts. Fill each insert two-thirds full with batter and place muffin pan in oven. Bake 20 minutes, or until a cake tester comes out clean from the center.

For garnish, drizzle cupcakes with melted chocolate and sprinkle with coconut, sunflower seeds, or your choice of topping.

Pistachio Baklava

(Dairy) Serves 4-6

Baklava:

3 cups pistachio nuts, shelled and chopped

½ cup raw cashew, chopped

½ cup sugar

1 teaspoon cinnamon

1 stick unsalted butter, melted

1 tablespoon olive oil

12 sheets phyllo dough

Syrup:

¾ cup water

1 cup sugar

3 tablespoons fresh lemon juice

Heat water and sugar until sugar completely dissolves. Add lemon juice and set aside to cool to room temperature.

Preheat oven to 375°F. Mix together pistachios, cashews, sugar and cinnamon. Mix in 4 tablespoons of syrup and set aside. Mix together butter and oil. Lay one sheet of phyllo on a lightly flour-covered surface and gently brush with butter-oil mixture. Top with a second phyllo sheet and again gently brush with butter-oil mixture. Repeat process with six sheets of phyllo, making a stack. Place nut mixture along one long edge of phyllo stack and roll into a cylinder. Repeat process for a second baklava roll. Transfer rolls to a lightly greased baking sheet and place on lowest rack of oven. Bake 10-15 minutes, until golden brown. When cool, slice each roll into 4-6 pieces, drizzle with remaining syrup, and serve with coffee.

Rosh HaShanah

Speak unto the children of Israel, saying: In the seventh month, in the first day of the month, shall be a solemn rest unto you, a memorial proclaimed with the blast of horns, a holy convocation.

—LEVITICUS 23:24

Rosh HaShanah, the Jewish New Year, is a celebration urging people to engage in spiritual reflection, repentance and worship. The holiday falls on the 1st and 2nd of Tishrei. Tishrei is not the first month of the Jewish calendar, but the seventh. The spring month of Nisan is considered the first month, near Passover.

Yamim Noraim (Days of Awe) officially begins with Rosh HaShanah and ends ten days later with Yom Kippur. Rosh HaShanah is the beginning of the time period called the High Holy Days.

In the Bible, other names used for Rosh HaShanah are Yom HaZikaron (Day of Remembrance) and Yom Teruah (Day of Blasts). The shofar (horn of a ram), blown similarly to a trumpet, is one of the highlights of the holiday. To understand the sounds of the shofar, one must consider several parts of the Bible. The reading of the Torah for Rosh HaShanah is the near sacrifice of Isaac by Abraham. A ram provided by God is substituted as the sacrifice. The near sacrifice of his son was a test of Abraham's loyalty to God, a type of judgment day. The shofar sound was emitted at Mt. Sinai as God revealed the Aseret HaDibrot (Ten Commandments). The sound of the shofar brought down the ancient walls of Jericho during the return of the Israelites to the Promised Land. As God reviews our actions over the year and judges His creation, Jews engage in acts of *tzedakah* (justice or charity), *tefilla* (prayer), and *t'shuva* (repentance).

Stunningly, the blasts of the shofar are meant to encourage us to repent and to connect to God. The non-verbal essence of the service teaches us that God understands and accepts our words, our actions, and even our cries. The blasts are systematic. The *tekiah* is a single long blast with a clear tone, a loud command; the *shevarim* is a series of three short blasts, similar to a person who is overcome with unexpected emotion; the *teruah* is a rapid series of very short blasts, a more thought out cry; and the *tekiah gedolah*,

the great *tekiah*, is the longest and the last blast of the shofar. Each blast is a cry to reach out to God. God speaks to us through the shofar service.

One of the beautiful traditions that has developed around the holiday is the Rosh HaShanah seder. Eating apples with honey, and a round challah dipped in honey, symbolically express wishes for a sweet New Year.

The special round challah used on all Yom Tovim (Torah-based Holy Days) reminds us of the circular nature of the yearly Jewish calendar. A special tradition is to include sweet things inside of the challah, such as chocolate, raisins, or other dried fruit. Honey is often used as a condiment for the Rosh HaShanah challah.

The apple has been compared to the fruit that Eve ate and gave to Adam which brings us to confront Judaism's view on creation. The apple is sweetened again with honey because we celebrate creation, the birthday of the world, a main feature of Rosh HaShanah.

The rimon (pomegranate) is a fruit mentioned in the Torah. In Israel, it tends to be ripe during the time of Rosh HaShanah. The seeds inside of the fruit are reminiscent of great fertility. Another reason given for blessing and eating pomegranate on Rosh HaShanah is that we hope for our good deeds in the coming year to be as plentiful as the seeds of the pomegranate.

Fish is eaten as an appetizer on Rosh HaShanah and is significant on several levels. The sages noted that fish never shut their eyes, just as God does not shut His anthropomorphic eyes. And just as fish never sleep, we hope to maintain a constant awareness of our mission in life and to remain aware of God's expectations at all times. The fish lays many eggs, another suggestion of fertility, and also abundance and prosperity. A fish head is often eaten, accompanied by the blessing, "May we be like a head (leader) and not a tail (follower)."

Peace Dove

An effective way to understand this holiday is to study the greetings said before, during and after Rosh HaShanah—*L'Shanah Tovah*, "A good year;" *L'Shanah Tovah U'metukah*, "A good sweet New Year;" *L'Shanah Tovah Tikatevu*, "May you be inscribed (in the Book of Life) for a good year;" and *G'mar Chatimah Tovah*, "May you finish with a good signature," though this last greeting is used mainly during Yom Kippur. The fascinating traditions that have developed around the holidays are an example of the vitality of Judaism because it has adapted over the centuries to move from a mainly Temple-based practice to one that takes place in Jewish homes and synagogues. These greetings tell of our aspirations to central prayer for the High Holidays, the U'netana Tokef, where God is viewed as a Judge, King and source of compassion. All Jews are seen by God, and He decides who will be inscribed in the Book of Life, or who will die. The decree can be softened by acts of charity, prayer and repentance during the Days of Awe.

Table Description

This table has a theme of purity and white. The crystal charger evokes sophistication. The silver plate and silver rimmed wine glasses state the graceful style of the holiday paired with the fine napkins matching the elegant tablecloth. The centerpiece is a bouquet of white flowers which connects the theme of sterling, white and beauty to the silver napkin holders that act as perches for decorative doves, representing peace. A shofar and a collection of apples remind us of the traditions of Rosh HaShanah. A lovely embellishment for the table setting is a heart-shaped honey bottle with a place card attached, which is also intended to be a gift for the guests.

This is a time for wishing one another a sweet New Year, and for the traditional blessing, "May your name be inscribed in the Book of Life." It is a time to forgive and open a new page. And it's a great opportunity to ask God to help you this year with all you need.

Involving the Children

Making greeting cards is a long-held tradition to prepare for the High Holy Days. A card made by a child is a much loved gift for relatives and family friends. Another activity for the children is to make a pomegranate out of self-drying clay which can then be painted bright red. A holiday gift for the children is to put ingredients for a honey cake in a mason jar, along with directions on how to prepare and cook the cake. The jar can be decorated with the Rosh HaShanah greeting of your choice.

Sweet Dipped Apple

Surprise your guests with sweet apples dipped in different flavors: marshmallow, chocolate, nuts, honey, candy, or whatever inspires you. Honey servers or pretzel sticks complete these delightful treats.

Turban Challah with Raisins or Chocolate Chips

(Pareve) Makes two challah

5 cups all purpose flour

1 tablespoon instant yeast

2 eggs, beaten lightly

⅓ cup canola oil

¼ cup honey

⅓ cup sugar

1 tablespoon salt

¾ cup raisins or chocolate chips

1½ cups warm water

1 egg, beaten with 1 tablespoon water

4 tablespoons honey

2 tablespoons boiling water

Preheat oven to 350°F. Combine ingredients, flour to raisins/chocolate chips. Using mixer on low speed, slowly add water. Increase to high speed and mix for several minutes until well blended. Let dough rest for 45 minutes. Knead dough on a lightly flour-covered surface until soft. Divide dough in half. Shape each half into 36″ strands. Coil each strand into lightly greased 9″ round cake pans. Cover challah with plastic wrap and kitchen towel and let rise until it fills the pan, approximately 1 hour. Brush challah with egg wash. Bake 20-25 minutes or until golden brown.

Mix honey and water until well blended. Brush on top of hot challah.

Applicious

Table Description

A white Battenberg lace tablecloth is the setting for this rosy Rosh HaShanah table. A shofar (ram's horn) and machzor (prayer book) are placed on the table to commemorate the holiday.

Ruby red chargers are topped with fluted white dinner and salad plates, with a bright red napkin positioned between the plates. A small plastic bee is placed next to a candied apple, using a honey server for the stick.

Red wine glasses reflect the red of the apples piled high in the two hurricane vases surrounding the centerpiece. The centerpiece is a third hurricane vase filled with slices of apples and red and white flowers, and a red bowl of apple slices is nearby for guests to nibble on. A tall decanter is filled with red wine, and candle holders with an apple base provide ambience for the evening.

Sea Bass on a Bed of Green

(Pareve) Serves 4-6

2 small whole sea bass or
 1½ pounds of sea bass fillets

5½ tablespoons olive oil, divided

¾ cup white wine

6 garlic cloves, peeled and chopped

4 sprigs fresh thyme

6 tablespoons lemon juice, divided

Salt and ground pepper

2 bunches baby spinach (or other
 greens, such as rainbow swiss chard),
 chopped into ½″ pieces

1 pound kale

3 tablespoons balsamic vinegar

1 teaspoon sugar

¼ cup toasted almonds

½ red bell pepper, seeds removed
 and chopped

Pre-heat oven to 400°F. Wash and dry fish. Cut a slit in fillet to create a pocket that is open on one side only. In a large glass baking dish, mix together 4 tablespoons oil, wine, garlic, thyme, and 2 tablespoons lemon juice, adding salt and pepper to taste. Add fish and marinate 15 minutes on each side. Stuff fish with spinach mixed with 2 tablespoons lemon juice. Put fish in oven and cook for 12 minutes on each side, or until fully cooked without becoming too dry.

In a sauté pan, cook kale with 1½ tablespoons olive oil. Once kale has cooked down, add balsamic vinegar, 2 tablespoons lemon juice, and sugar. Continue to sauté kale until slightly crisp, about 4 minutes. Place kale on serving platter and top with fish. Garnish with toasted almonds and red bell peppers.

Grilled Japanese Eggplant in Spicy Honey
(Pareve) Serves 4-6

6 Japanese eggplants, cut in half lengthwise

2 tablespoons canola oil

3 garlic cloves, peeled and minced

1 teaspoon chili paste

2 tablespoons fresh ginger, peeled and grated

5 tablespoons clover honey

Juice of 1 lemon

3 tablespoons water

Salt and pepper

Preheat grill. Brush each eggplant half with oil and cook on grill until lightly brown on both sides. In a sauté pan, brown garlic in a little oil and stir in chili paste, ginger, honey and lemon juice. Add enough water to turn the paste into a sauce. Add grilled eggplant into the mixture, cut side down. Allow to simmer for 10 minutes or until all the sauce has been absorbed by the eggplant. Season with salt and pepper to taste.

A Sweet New Year

The prayer book for Rosh HaShanah is specifically designed for the holiday. It includes many piyutim (poems) recorded through the ages that reflect the sacredness of God and set the mood for considering our own relationship to Him. The High Holy Day Prayer Book is called a machzor (cycle). A major theme describes God as the Creator and we are the created, in a similar way that God is like a potter and we are His clay.

Table Description

A simple white tablecloth sets the scene for a celebration of apples and honey. Stoneware plates featuring apple artwork are placed on green chargers. Folded white napkins are secured with crown napkin rings. Iridescent green glass goblets and a green glass vase draw in the green accents on the plates. The centerpiece looks impressive, and it might look difficult to create, but it is actually a simple process. Use a donut shaped piece of floral foam and simply skewer small apples along the sides. Add roses to the foam, right up to the hole in the center. Place a glass jar in the hole and fill it with honey sticks. Finally, place a machzor and a shofar on the table to remind your guests that this is the Rosh HaShanah holiday.

Chicken with Sweet Potatoes

(Meat) Serves 6-8

Chicken, cut into 8 pieces
  (do not remove skin)

6 small-medium sweet potatoes,
  peeled and cut into quarters

15 small shallots or onions

12 pitted prunes, dried black

Pre-heat oven to 375°F. Mix together
all sauce ingredients. Place chicken into
a big pot with skin facing up. Add
sweet potatoes, onions and prunes.
Pour sauce over chicken and cover pan
with foil. Set aside for at least 3 hours.
Bake covered for 1½ hours. Remove
cover and bake an additional 30 minutes.

Sauce:

½ cup honey

½ cup soy sauce

4 tablespoons balsamic vinegar

4 tablespoons olive oil

¾ cup dry red wine

4 garlic cloves, peeled and
  finely chopped

1 tablespoon coriander seeds, lightly
  crushed (or ground coriander)

2 bay leaves

5 sprigs fresh thyme

2 cinnamon sticks (optional)

Salt and pepper

Sweet and Sour Red Cabbage

(Pareve) Serves 6-8

½ stick margarine

6 cups red cabbage, thinly sliced

4 tablespoons sugar

2-3 tablespoons balsamic vinegar

Juice of 1 lemon

Salt and pepper

¼ cup roasted and salted sunflower seeds (optional)

Melt margarine in large pot over medium heat. Add cabbage and sauté 5 minutes, or until slightly wilted. Add sugar and toss to coat evenly. Reduce heat to medium-low. Add vinegar and simmer 25 minutes, stirring often, until cabbage is tender. Season to taste with lemon juice, salt and pepper. If desired, add sunflower seeds.

May you be inscribed and sealed for a good year.

Time Change

On Rosh HaShanah we eat special foods symbolic of New Year blessings, including a piece of apple dipped in honey, symbolizing our desire for a sweet year. We bless one another with the words, *L'Shanah Tovah Tikatevu*, "May you be inscribed (in the Book of Life) for a good year."

Table Description

This table is decorated in green and white, signs of growth and a new beginning. The theme of this table is found in the hourglasses, symbolizing the end of the past year and the beginning of a New Year. Two green runners, embroidered with flowers, are crossed on a pure white tablecloth with green plates placed on the runners. Each plate holds a cupcake decorated with the image of bees on a beehive, symbolizing honey and wishes for a sweet New Year. The hourglasses are placed at the side of each plate to remind us that the year is changing. The centerpiece is a deep glass bowl with small green apples in the bottom and yellow flowers on top, complementing the yellow of the cupcake.

Tripolitan Semolina Cake

(Pareve) Serves 4-6

2 eggs

1 cup canola oil

2 teaspoons vanilla extract

1½ cups fresh squeezed orange juice

Zest of 1 orange

1 cup sugar

4 cups semolina flour

2½ tablespoons baking powder

1 cup unsweetened dried coconut

1½ cups almonds, finely chopped

½ cup golden raisins (optional)

Whole almonds

Syrup:

½ cup water

½ tablespoon fresh squeezed lemon juice

1 cups sugar

Preheat oven to 350°F. Mix together eggs, oil, vanilla, orange juice, orange zest and sugar. In a separate bowl mix together flour, baking powder, coconut and almonds. Create a well in dry ingredients and add wet ingredients. Stir thoroughly until well blended. Mix in raisins (optional).

Pour batter into a greased 9″ x 9″ square pan. Score batter into squares or diamonds. Garnish each piece with a whole almond. Bake for 35 minutes, or until a cake tester comes out clean from the center. Allow cake to cool.

Before serving, mix together water, lemon juice and sugar. Heat on medium heat. Allow to come to a simmer and continue to cook until a nice golden color. Cut cake into squares or diamonds and pour syrup over the entire cake, reserving enough syrup to drizzle over cake slices before serving.

Note: It is important to pour hot syrup over a cool cake.

Shalom Rosh HaShanah

On the afternoon of Rosh HaShanah, a ceremony called Tashlich (to cast off) is conducted that emphasizes the special relationship between God and humanity. It is a time to reflect on one's mistakes/sins. After the sounding of the shofar, Jewish families symbolically cast off their sins by tossing crumbs into a body of water: a river, a lake, or an ocean. Tashlich portrays the sincere desire to heal our relationship with God, and serves as a crucial part in the process of repenting and returning to God in purity.

Table Description

Because we renew our relationship with God on Rosh HaShanah, the napkin rings and centerpiece on this stunning table feature crowns for the Ruler of the Universe. The crown-shaped vase centerpiece holds water that is tinted red with food coloring, highlighting the red of the flowers. The centerpiece has artificial doves attached, representing the peace that we desire in the New Year. Crystal candlesticks accent the white and silver table and silver chargers give a unique ruffled appearance to each place setting. Crystal stemware and a decanter of wine completes an elegant and memorable table for your New Year celebration. L'Shanah Tovah!

Apple Strudel

(Pareve) Serves 4-6

Filling:

4 tablespoons margarine

5 large Granny Smith apples, peeled and cut into small squares

1 teaspoon cinnamon

3-4 tablespoons sugar

Zest of ½ lemon

4 tablespoons walnuts or almonds, coarsely crushed

½ tablespoon lemon juice

1½ tablespoon sweet red wine (optional)

Strudel:

5 tablespoons almond crumbs

5 tablespoons powdered sugar

1 teaspoon cinnamon

¼ cup margarine, melted

4 sheets phyllo dough

Powdered sugar for garnish

Filling: Melt margarine in sauté pan over low heat. Add apples and cook 3 minutes. Add cinnamon, sugar and lemon zest. Stir and cook an additional 3 minutes. Add walnuts or almonds, lemon juice and, if desired, red wine, and bring to a boil. Cook over medium heat for 2 more minutes. Drain apples well and let cool.

Strudel: Preheat oven to 375°F. Mix together almond crumbs, powdered sugar and cinnamon. Brush margarine over a phyllo sheet and then spread with almond crumbs mixture. Repeat process, creating a four-layer stack, using only melted margarine on the top sheet. Place phyllo stack on greased baking sheet. Cut into 4-6 squares. Add apple-nut filling into center of each square stack. Bring each corner of the square stack up, twisting at the top and creating a "purse." Brush the top of each stack with margarine. Place baking sheet on lowest oven rack. Bake 30 minutes, or until golden brown and crisp. Sprinkle with powdered sugar. Serve with any flavor of sorbet.

Celebrating the Mitzvot for the New Year

Table Description

A red tablecloth and a table runner decorated with pomegranates beautifully displays the centerpiece of intertwined shofars surrounded by gold and deep red apples. Golden chargers embrace the pomegranate patterned plates, with bone-handled cutlery at each place setting. Golden wine glasses and candleholders further enhance the golden colors of the chargers and table runner. Burgundy wine in a glass decanter highlights the deep colors of the shofar and apple centerpiece, while a bowl of pomegranates duplicates the design of the table runner and patterned plates. The addition of the machzor completes the traditional symbols for Rosh HaShanah.

"And this shall be an everlasting statute unto you, to make atonement for the children of Israel because of all their sins once in the year." And he did as the LORD commanded Moses.

—LEVITICUS 16:34

Yom Kippur

Yom Kippur is the holiest day of the year. According to Jewish tradition, on Rosh HaShanah God inscribes each person's fate for the coming year into a book, the Book of Life. He then waits until Yom Kippur to "seal" the verdict. During the Days of Awe, the ten days after Rosh HaShanah leading up to Yom Kippur, a Jewish person tries to amend his or her behavior and seek forgiveness for wrongs done against God (*bein adam LeMakom*) and against other human beings (*bein adam lechavero*). The evening and day of Yom Kippur are set aside for public and private petitions and confessions of guilt (*vidui*).

This High Holy Day is also known as the Day of Atonement, when we draw close to God and reflect on the ideal state of our souls. Because of our own faults and shortcomings, we must afflict our souls on this day as Leviticus 16:29-30 directs. Jewish people traditionally observe a 25-hour period of fasting and intensive prayer, often spending most of the day in synagogue services. Acts of charity are performed as additional good deeds (*mitzvot*).

...in the seventh month, on the tenth day of the month, ye shall afflict your souls, and shall do no manner of work...For on this day shall atonement be made for you, to cleanse you; from all your sins shall ye be clean before the LORD.

—LEVITICUS 16:29-30

Although the focus is the complete fast, the day is commemorated with festive meals: one before the fast begins, and one to break the fast. As always, any of these restrictions can be lifted when a threat to life or health is involved. In fact, children under the age of nine and women in childbirth (from the time labor begins until three days after birth) are not permitted to fast, even if they want to. Older children and women who have recently given birth (from the third to seventh day after childbirth) are permitted to fast, but are permitted to break the fast if they feel the need to do so. People with any illnesses should consult a physician and rabbi for advice.

And Aaron shall lay both his hands upon the head of the live goat, and confess over him all the iniquities of the children of Israel, and all their transgressions, even all their sins; and he shall put them upon the head of the goat, and shall send him away by the hand of an appointed man into the wilderness.

—LEVITICUS 16:21

Kaparot

In preparation for Yom Kippor, the kaparot ("atonement") ceremony is performed. This consists of waving a chicken three times over one's head while reciting traditional text. After the chicken is slaughtered, either its monetary value is given to the poor or the chicken itself is donated to charity. We ask God to transfer to this chicken any evil/sin decree over our heads so that we start the new year with a clean slate.

One reason suggested for the choice of a chicken to perform the kaparot rite is because it is not a species that was eligible for offering as a sacrifice in the Holy Temple. This helps prevent any conclusion that the kaparot is a sacrifice. If a chicken is unavailable, one may substitute another kosher fowl (besides a dove or pigeon, as they were offered as sacrifices in the Holy Temple). Some use a kosher live fish; others perform the entire rite with money and then give the money to charity.

Table Description

This colorful and happy table describes the relief that comes from being rid of all our sins. Colorful rooster print plates are vibrant against a white tablecloth, and beautifully complement the centerpiece with three roosters. Napkins with feather napkin rings placed by each plate complete the presentation of the kaparot tradition. Candlesticks and candles integrate well with the colors of the table, and add to the festive atmosphere.

Because Yom Kippur is the highest Holy Day of the year and there is no work on this day, preparation is important; thus, the key for hosting is simplicity. Carefully pre-plan your menu, what you will eat and drink before and after the fast. The pre-fast meal should be satisfying, but not so heavy that it will become a distraction later in the evening.

Involving the Children

A few days before Yom Kippur, gather the children to design kippot (prayer head covers) for each male guest and to prepare refreshing scented apples to be used by those fasting. Each child can decorate a white kippa and then write the name of the guest on it. The kippa will be on the table waiting for the guest. This little bit of attention from the children will make the guests feel welcome. Children can prepare the apples by pressing in whole cloves all over, which creates a spicy aroma to help the guests manage the fast more easily. (My grandmother, whom I love so much, prepared clove apples, and I helped her. It was fun to do, and the subtle aroma throughout the day really helped me to get through the fast.)

Pre-fast Delight

The Yom Kippur prayer service includes several unique aspects. One is the actual number of prayer services (Ma'ariv, Shacharit, Musaf, Mincha and Ne'ilah, the closing prayer). The prayer services also include private and public confessions of sins (vidui) and a unique prayer dedicated to the special avodah (service) of the Kohen Gadol (High Priest) in the Holy Temple in Jerusalem. As one of the most culturally significant Jewish holidays, Yom Kippur is observed by many secular Jews who may not observe other holidays. Many secular Jews attend synagogue on Yom Kippur and for many secular Jews, the High Holy Days are the only recurring times of the year in which they attend synagogue, causing synagogue attendance to soar. Yom means "day" in Hebrew and Kippur comes from the root that means "to atone." Thus Yom Kippur has come to mean the Day of Atonement. Some say there is a link to kaparot, the "mercy seat" or covering, of the Ark of the Covenant. Abraham Ibn Ezra states that the word indicates the task and not just the shape of the Ark cover. Since the blood of the Yom Kippur sacrifice was sprinkled in its direction, it was the symbol of propitiation.

Table Description

Set in the temple against the background of colorfully dressed Torah scrolls, this pre-fast table is decorated in blue, white and green. Delicate blue wine glasses and square white plates top a bold blue-and-white striped tablecloth. Green apples decorated with fragrant whole cloves make an attractive presentation in the center of the plates. After dinner, each guest may use their fragrant apple to comfort themselves during the fast. At the side of each plate is a napkin with a blue and white Star of David print. The centerpiece for the table is an alabaster glass wine decanter. A single votive candle holder with flourishes of lavender flowers and a white ribbon sheds light from its high perch. A shofar and tallit lying on the table remind all the guests of the essence of Yom Kippur, the holy day being observed.

Meat or Potato Bourekas with Mushroom Sauce

(Meat or Pareve) Serves 6-8

3 tablespoons canola oil

1 large onion, finely chopped

3 cloves garlic, peeled and minced
(for meat filling)

2 cups mushrooms, chopped
(for potato filling)

1 pound ground meat or
5 potatoes, peeled, boiled and mashed

2 tablespoons chicken bouillon powder
(or mushroom powder, for potato filling only)

1 cup pine nuts

½ cup cilantro, chopped

¼ cup parsley, chopped

Pinch of sweet pepper (optional)

Pinch of tumeric (optional)

Salt and pepper

1 package frozen puff pastry, thawed

1 egg, beaten with 1 tablespoon water

Sesame seeds

Mushroom Sauce:

2 teaspoons canola oil

1 large onion, finely chopped

1 15 oz. can sliced mushrooms, rinsed and drained

2 tablespoons flour

1½ cups chicken broth

2 tablespoons mushroom powder

2 tablespoons fresh parsley, chopped

Black pepper

Hot water, as needed

Meat Filling:

Heat oil in medium pan. Add onion and garlic, cooking until golden. Add meat, crumbling with fork to avoid clumps. Continue cooking until meat is done, removing any excess juices. Add bouillon powder, pine nuts, cilantro, parsley and seasonings to taste. Stirring occasionally, cook a few more minutes until well incorporated.

Potato Filling:

Heat oil in medium pan. Add onion, cooking until golden. Add mushrooms, cooking until soft. In a medium bowl, mix together mashed potatoes, onion-mushroom mixture, chicken bouillon or mushroom powder, pine nuts, cilantro, parsley, and seasonings to taste.

Pastry:

Pre-heat oven to 325°F. On a lightly flour-covered surface, cut each sheet of puff pastry into 6 equal squares to give 12 squares in total. Brush edges of each square lightly with egg wash. Place a heaping tablespoon of the meat or potato mixture in the center of each square. Fold pastry over the filling to form a triangle, and seal edges with a fork. Transfer pastry to lightly greased baking sheet. Brush with remaining egg wash and sprinkle with sesame seeds. Bake 20-30 minutes, until golden brown. Serve immediately with mushroom sauce poured over top or served on the side.

Mushroom Sauce:

Heat oil in medium pan. Add onion, cooking until golden. Add mushrooms, cooking until soft. Add flour, evenly coating onions and mushrooms. Add chicken broth, mushroom powder, parsley and black pepper to taste. Reduce heat and stir often until sauce is thickened. Add hot water if sauce becomes too thick.

New Beginnings

And he shall make atonement for the holy place,
because of the uncleannesses of the children of Israel,
and because of their transgressions, even all their sins;
and so shall he do for the tent of meeting, that
dwelleth with them in the midst of their uncleannesses.

—LEVITICUS 16:16

It is customary to wear white on Yom Kippur, which also symbolizes purity, and calls to mind the promise that our sins shall be made as white as snow. In order to apologize to God, one must do three mitzvot: prayer, repentance and charity.

Prayer services begin with the Kol Nidrei prayer, which must be recited before sunset, and continue with the evening prayers (Ma'ariv or Arvith), which include an extended Selichot service. The concluding service of Yom Kippur, known as Ne'ilah, "closing" prayer, begins shortly before sunset. The ark (a cabinet for the scrolls of the Torah) is kept open throughout this service; thus you must stand throughout the service. There is a tone of desperation in the prayers of this service, sometimes referred to as the closing of the gates; think of it as the "last chance" to get in a good word before the holiday ends. A recitation of Shema Yisrael and the blowing of the shofar mark the end of the fast. The service ends with a very long blast of the shofar.

Table Description

All white can make a table setting look inviting, while at the same time continuing the theme of "refreshment" and "new beginnings." White glows with the promise of fresh starts, purity and memorial candle-lighting that are traditional observations on Yom Kippur. Crystal wine glasses bring even more elegance to the white plates on gracefully stylish beaded chargers. Vases with white tulips and crystal beads create the centerpiece. On the table sit salt-and-pepper shakers shaped like two bunches of grapes; the scale-like design symbolizes the time that God will weigh our good deeds against our bad.

Chicken with Peas

(Meat) Serves 6-8

2 tablespoons canola oil

2 large onions, sliced into moon shapes

Chicken, divided into 8 pieces

1 tablespoon cumin

2 tablespoons turmeric

1 teaspoon sweet paprika

Salt and pepper

2½ cups frozen peas

2 bay leaves

1 bunch fresh dill, chopped

½ cup fresh cilantro, chopped

½ cup fresh parsley, chopped

4 cups chicken broth

Water, as needed

Heat oil in large pot and fry onion until light brown. Add chicken, cumin, turmeric, sweet paprika, and salt and pepper to taste. Fry until golden, approximately 2-3 minutes per side. Add peas, bay leaves, and half each of dill, cilantro and parsley. Mix together. Add broth to cover chicken, adding water if needed. Bring to boil, lower heat and cover. Cook on low heat for 45 minutes. Check periodically and add water as needed to keep chicken covered. When chicken is cooked through, add remaining dill, cilantro and parsley. Let sit for several minutes to allow additional spices to be absorbed for flavor.

Chocolate Balls

(Pareve) Makes 8-12 balls

½ cup high-quality dark chocolate

3 tablespoons margarine

3 cups shredded coconut

5 tablespoons sugar

3 tablespoons cocoa powder

½ cup water

3 cups tea biscuits, ground

½ tablespoon vanilla extract

2-3 tablespoons walnuts, chopped

1-2 tablespoons Irish liquor (optional)

Melt chocolate and margarine in a double boiler. Place coconut in a deep bowl and set aside. In a separate bowl, mix together remaining ingredients. Add melted chocolate and mix well. Shape dough into round balls. Roll each ball in coconut, covering the entire ball. Refrigerate 3 hours and serve cold.

"A good and blessed year."

For on this day shall atonement be made for you, to cleanse you; from all your sins shall ye be clean before the LORD.

—LEVITICUS 16:30

Yom Kippur is a complete Sabbath; no work may be performed on that day. It is well known that on Yom Kippur you are to refrain from eating and drinking (even water), beginning before sunset on the eve of Yom Kippur and ending at sundown on Yom Kippur. The Talmud also specifies additional restrictions that are less well known: washing and bathing, anointing one's body (with cosmetics, deodorants, etc.), wearing leather shoes (Orthodox Jews routinely wear canvas sneakers with their dress clothes on Yom Kippur), and acts of intimacy are all prohibited on Yom Kippur.

As we leave the synagogue at the end of Yom Kippur, we bless each other by exchanging wishes for "a good and blessed year."

Table Description

A pitcher of mint tea is very good for aiding digestion. It is recommended to drink this before and after the fast. On the table, place napkins with napkin holders shaped like Stars of David. Add a feather pen on the High Holy Day prayer book, the machzor. The book with the feather pen symbolizes the hope of everyone to be written in the Book of Life and to start a new, clean beginning.

Sukkot

Sukkot

Speak unto the children of Israel, saying:
On the fifteenth day of this seventh month
is the feast of tabernacles for seven days
unto the LORD.

—LEVITICUS 23:34

Like all Jewish holidays, Sukkot (Festival of Booths) has certain main components, including the historical and spiritual practices of the Israelites. God instructed the Jewish people to construct booths: *Ye shall dwell in booths seven days; all that are home-born in Israel shall dwell in booths* (Leviticus 23:42). Sukkot celebrates how the Israelites followed God into the desert, certain that God would watch over them. In doing so, this band of newly freed slaves showed their faith in God. As the Israelites traveled in the wilderness, they lived in temporary structures. The sukkah, or booth, is a symbol to remind us of our time in the wilderness. The spiritual component focuses on living outside, and there are specific laws about the structure. The roof of the sukkah is designed to provide more shade than sunlight and is meant to allow people to see the stars above. On Shimini Atzeret, the last day of the festival, Jews recite special prayers for rain.

Sukkot is one of the shalosh regalim, three pilgrimage holidays ordained in the Torah. All Israelites were commanded to come to Jerusalem on Sukkot and to set up their temporary home. The sukkah still has significance for Jews today as it reminds us that during our own lives in this world we rely on God's providence to protect us.

Table Description

Yellow and bright green are two colors associated with Sukkot, and they reflect the hues of the etrog, a medium-sized citrus fruit, and the foliage and fruit in the lulav, which is a handful of branches mentioned in Scripture to celebrate this harvest festival. The view outdoors gives the guests the impression of being in a sukkah. Fresh flowers add to the sense of joy of trusting God for provision day-by-day. On each plate lays a half lemon with the fruit scooped out and replaced by a bouquet of flowers. This arrangement adds beauty to the table by affecting our sense of smell, sight, and touch.

You will dwell in booths for seven days; all natives of Israel shall dwell in booths.

—LEVITICUS 23:42

A large tray may be used to move the food and other items from the kitchen to the sukkah. Children can help by loading their wagons with whatever will fit to provide everything needed for the sukkah.

Involving the Children

In decorating the sukkah, inspiration can be found in almost any component of the holiday. The Four Species (four plants mentioned in the Torah) are held together with a straw band. The children can make straw bands as napkin rings to represent the Four Species. They can also weave leaves together to make a placemat for the guests visiting the sukkah. Artwork is beautiful and when a child sees his or her work proudly displayed in the sukkah, it makes it their own. Finally, one of the best things for children to do during Sukkot is to ask their friends over to visit the sukkah and enjoy refreshments, activities, and even a sleep over, if possible.

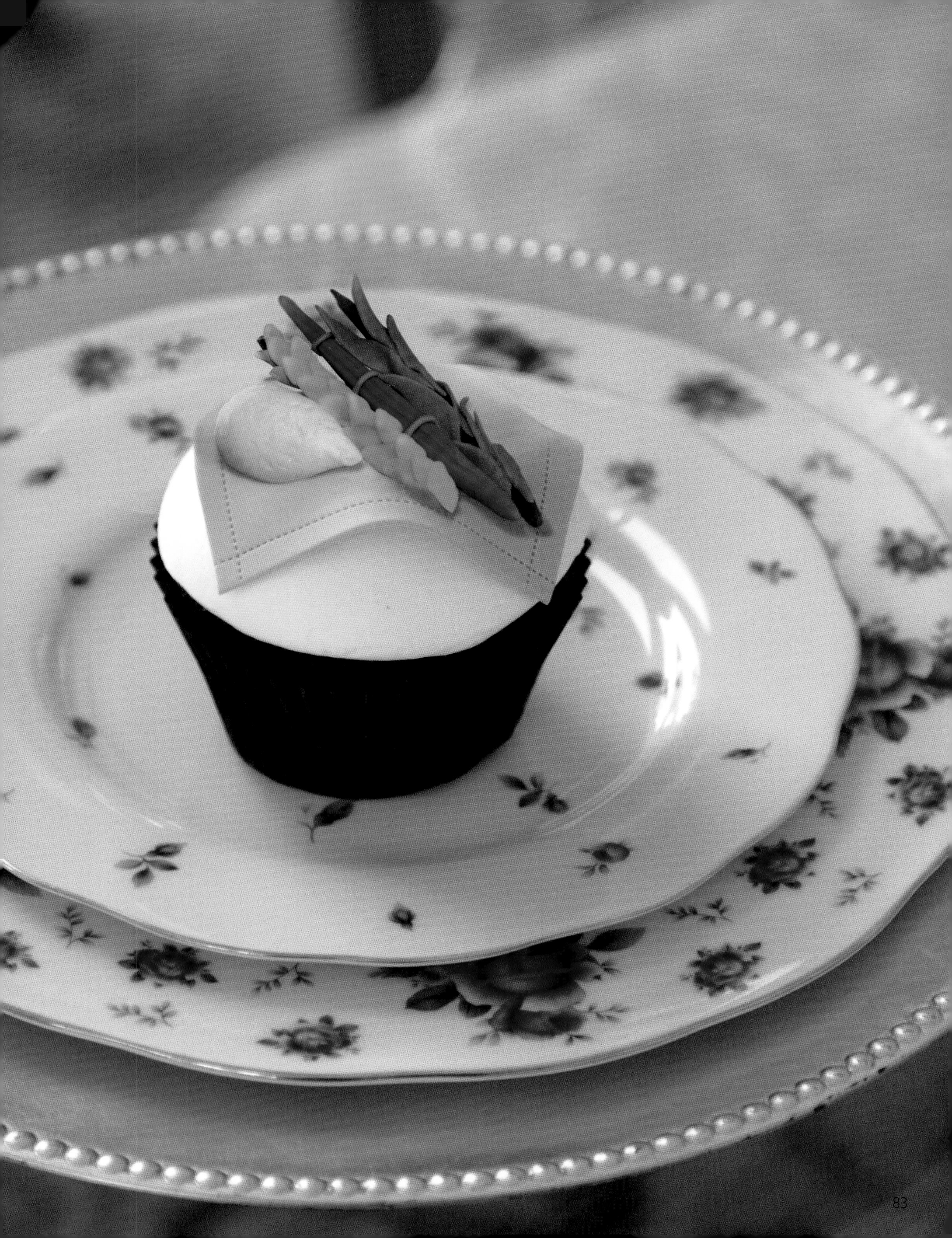

Tagine of Chicken, Olives, Lemon and Mushrooms

(Meat) Serves 6-8

¼ cup olive oil

2 medium onions, chopped

6 garlic cloves, peeled and sliced

2 tablespoons mushroom powder

3 tablespoons olive tapenade spread

1 chicken, cut into 8 pieces

4 tablespoons fresh lemon juice, divided

Salt and pepper

1-1½ cups chicken broth or water

3 cups button mushrooms

1 cup leeks, chopped (only use white and light green parts)

1 tablespoon cumin

1 tablespoon turmeric

1 cup pitted green and Kalamata olives, whole

½ cup fresh parsley, chopped

½ cup fresh cilantro, chopped

12 small potatoes, peeled (optional)

Heat oil in sauté pan or tagine and sauté onion and garlic for 4 minutes, until golden. Add mushroom powder and olive tapenade spread and mix together. Season chicken with 2 tablespoons lemon juice and salt and pepper to taste. Add chicken broth or water, chicken pieces, mushrooms, leeks, cumin and turmeric. Mix all together and cook, covered, on medium heat for 25 minutes. Add olives, remaining lemon juice, and ¼ cup each of parsley and cilantro. Mix all together, and bring to a boil. Cover and reduce heat to low for 30-40 minutes, until chicken is cooked through.

While cooking, gently stir the ingredients, and baste the chicken with the sauce at the bottom of the pan. Remove chicken to platter and garnish with remaining parsley and cilantro.

Note: You may also add slices of potatoes or 12 small potatoes to this recipe.

The Four Species

And ye shall take you on the first day the fruit of goodly trees, branches of palm-trees, and boughs of thick trees, and willows of the brook, and ye shall rejoice before the LORD your God seven days.

—LEVITICUS 23:40

In the sukkah we make a special blessing holding an etrog and lulav. The citron, or etrog, has fragrance and taste and is akin to a person who knows and follows the Torah. The lulav includes branches of willow, myrtle and palm to teach us something about ourselves and the natural world. The willow has neither fragrance nor taste; the myrtle has fragrance, but no taste; and the palm has taste, but no fragrance. All together, the Four Species represent all Jews, those who know and follow Torah, and those who do not know or follow Torah. All are celebrated during Sukkot. According to the rabbis, another metaphor for the Four Species is that they represent different parts of the body which are used in tandem to worship God. The citron is shaped like a heart, the willow like lips, the myrtle is like eyes, and the palm is like a spine.

Table Description

This beautiful "table with a view" sports a tall centerpiece of branches that represent the etrog and lulav. Lemon blossoms are extremely fragrant and mix well with palm and myrtle cuttings. Willow cuttings can also be added to this tall arrangement. Imitating the lulav, yellow napkins are fan-folded and green napkins, rolled and folded in half, are placed in the center of the fan. The embroidered tablecloth enhances the citrus theme. Add a shiny dark brown charger to support the dinner plate with a lemon cluster design and the effect is complete.

Stuffed Artichoke Crowns

(Meat) Serves 4-6

2 14-ounce cans artichoke crowns
(found at your local kosher grocery)

1 pound ground beef

2 egg yolks

1 large yellow onion, grated

2 garlic cloves, peeled and minced

¼ cup Panko bread crumbs

¼ cup fresh parsley, chopped

¼ cup fresh cilantro, chopped

1 tablespoon turmeric

½ tablespoon sweet paprika

Salt and pepper

2 eggs, beaten with 2 tablespoons water

1 cup all purpose flour

½ cup canola oil

Sauce:

2¼ cups water

3 tablespoons tomato paste

2 cups crushed tomatoes with juice

3 garlic cloves, peeled and minced

¼ cup fresh parsley, chopped

¼ cup fresh cilantro, chopped

1 tablespoon sweet paprika

1 tablespoon turmeric

Salt and pepper

Garnish:

4 tablespoons parsley, coarsely chopped

Pine nuts

Mix together ground beef through cilantro. Season with turmeric, sweet paprika and salt and pepper to taste. Fill the hollow of each artichoke crown with ground beef mixture, slightly heaping. Refrigerate for 30 minutes. Dip artichoke in egg, then flour. Heat oil in large sauté pan and add artichokes in a single layer, frying for 2 minutes, carefully turning until golden brown on both sides. Remove from pan and set aside.

Remove excess oil from pan. Add all sauce ingredients and simmer 10 minutes. Return artichokes to pan with sauce. Bring to a boil and reduce heat. Simmer covered for 1 hour, periodically stirring sauce around artichokes and also spooning sauce over tops of artichokes.

Serve with white rice. Garnish with parsley and pine nuts.

Couscous with Eggplant and Zucchini

(Pareve) Serves 4-6

1 large eggplant, cut into large chunks

1 large zucchini, cut into large chunks

2-3 tablespoons olive oil

Salt and pepper

4 ounces quick cooking couscous, vegetable flavored

1 garlic clove, peeled and chopped

1 tablespoon fresh cilantro, chopped

1 tablespoon fresh parsley, chopped

1 tablespoon fresh mint, chopped

Preheat broiler to high heat. Toss eggplant and zucchini with olive oil, adding salt and pepper to taste. Place eggplant and zucchini in a single layer on a non-stick baking sheet. Broil until golden brown, 7-8 minutes, turning occasionally.

While vegetables are broiling, prepare couscous per package directions, adding garlic. When done, gently stir vegetables, cilantro, parsley and mint into hot couscous. Serve immediately, while still hot.

Dining in Sunlight

The additional names that refer to Sukkot provide a deeper understanding of the significance of the holiday:

Chag HaAsif
(FEAST OF GATHERING)

Farmers who had spent long days working in the fields could gaze upon their neatly bound sheaves of wheat and credit their success to their own hard work, but Chag HaAsif reminded them to thank God for their bounty. Even today, workers in every field might gaze at their paycheck and credit their success to their own hard work, but Chag HaAsif reminds them to thank God. Recognizing God's place at the center of our good fortune keeps egos in check during the good times and keeps despair in its place during the hard times.

Z'man Simchateinu
(SEASON OF OUR REJOICING)

Sukkot follows closely behind Yom Kippur, contrasting the most solemn holiday to the most joyous. The slate has been wiped clean and so we are especially capable of fulfilling the mitzvah of joy on Sukkot. At this time of year, we celebrate the Shekhinah, the presence of HaShem in the clouds that protected Israel on all sides and from above. The construction of the family sukkah is intended to be reminiscent of the fragile dwellings used when the Israelites wandered forty years in the desert, after their exodus from slavery in Egypt, until we entered the Promised Land.

Table Description

This quaint wicker table is set among glorious palm trees. As an outdoor arrangement, the local flora acts as part of the ambience for the holiday. Clusters of lemons and the yellow candles in green palm branch candleholders provide reminders of the lulav color theme. The candles are also practical when the sun sets and it is time to light them and enjoy the meal.

Date Cookies

(Pareve) Makes 20 cookies

Dough:

4 tablespoons coconut cream

2 eggs

1 cup margarine

⅓ cup sugar

3 cups all-purpose flour

¾ tablespoon baking powder

Powdered sugar

Date Spread:

2 cups pre-packaged date spread

½ cup walnuts, finely chopped

Preheat oven to 350°F. In a large bowl, mix together coconut cream, eggs, margarine and sugar until smooth. Add flour and baking powder, mixing until well blended. Gently massage dough until it is soft and pliable. Refrigerate for 30 minutes.

When chilled, divide dough into 3 parts. On a floured surface, roll out each part into a rectangle with a thickness of about ⅛-inch. Spread ⅓ of the date spread on each rectangle in a thin, even layer. Sprinkle with walnuts. Roll up tightly and place on a cookie sheet with baking paper.

Bake 30-35 minutes, or until golden brown. Cool completely and cut cookies into 2″ pieces using a serrated knife. Sprinkle liberally with powdered sugar.

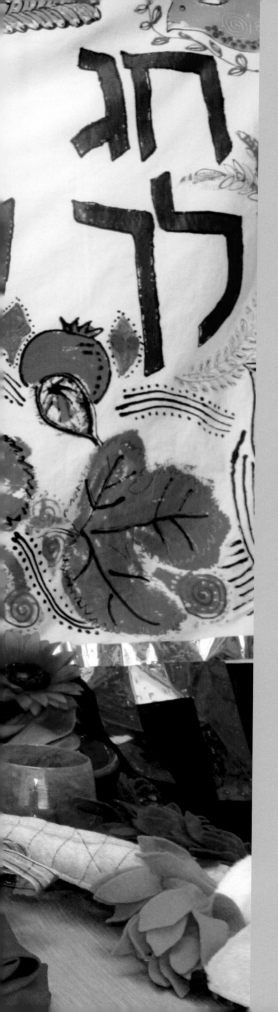

Ushpizin
(GUESTS)

There is a concept of beautifying the fulfillment of a commandment called Hidur Mitzvah. If one is able, it is meritorious to beautify the commandment. During a traditional Sukkot feast, in the sukkah we use beautiful dishes to serve the finest foods and invite friends and family, as well as mystical guests. Traditionally, Biblical figures are invited: Abraham, Isaac, Jacob, Joseph, Moses, Aaron and David. Inviting people of great importance is paralleled in Jewish liturgy where the worshiper mentions Abraham, Isaac, and Jacob to remind us of our relationship to our forefathers, and their connection to God. Essentially, the activity is geared to increase God's divine protection of the celebrants.

Table Description

This fall table abounds in autumn colors. The deep red candles and pomegranates suggest richness. The vase displays bright citrus yellow, contrasted with the green and red apples surrounded by palm leaves. The charger is made of a rustic woven dark brown material which contrasts the auburn and light green plates that they hold. The master napkin, folded like a leaf, is a subdued yellow, complementing the assembly of colorful plates. A flower with red petals and a maroon center rests on the leaf-shaped napkin, adding beauty and fragrance to the environment.

A Promising Dessert

For a dessert that will make your children smile, cut a lemon lengthwise, remove the fruit and scrape the rind until clean. Fill with sorbet and decorate with candies.

Palm Leaf Napkin Ring

Anyone can make a beautiful napkin ring using the leaf of a palm tree. Trim the leaf to a length of 6" x 2," shape into a circle and attach with hot glue. Fan-fold the napkin, then fold in half, and tuck the folded end into the napkin ring. Voila!

Chanukah

Blessed are You, LORD our God, King of the universe, who performed miracles for our ancestors in those days at this time.

Chanukah

Chanukah is a very special time for the Jewish people. Its beginnings tell of struggle and triumph spiritually and militarily, and it speaks to the modern Jew to encourage Jewish pride. The holiday is not found in the Bible due to its late occurrence. Chanukah means "dedication" and the original intent of the holiday was to celebrate the rededication of the Second Temple in Jerusalem after the defeat of the Greek Assyrians. Chanukah is also referred to as "The Festival of Lights" or Chag HaUrim. This name describes the main features of Chanukah, which involves the lighting of a nine-branched menorah, also known as a chanukiah. We celebrate Chanukah for eight days, from the 25th of Kislev, which usually falls during the month of November or December.

In addition to lighting the chanukiah, families gather together and celebrate by enjoying traditional foods, games and gifts, and by singing various songs that commemorate the rededication.

Foods cooked in oil (such as golden brown fresh jelly doughnuts and potato latkes) are eaten guilt-free. This is a small miracle itself, an opportunity to enjoy "naughty" foods. These foods represent the small amount of oil the Jews had available while defending the Temple when it was under siege centuries ago. Miraculously, the oil lasted for eight days instead of the single day it should have, the exact amount of time needed for fresh oil to be pressed and brought to the Temple. This is the miracle of Chanukah as most people know the story.

During the festival, the children play with a spinning top, called a dreidel. This wonderful game originated as a game of life or death. Because foreign powers did not allow Jews to study the Torah, the children had to learn in secret. If they were about to be discovered, they would quickly hide their books and pull out these small tops so they could pretend to be merely playing games, covering up their true purpose of gathering together.

Mogen David and Dreidels

Blessed are You, LORD our God, King of the universe, who has sanctified us with His commandments and commanded us to kindle the Chanukah light[s].

Table Description

This table setting presents all the essentials for celebrating the holiday. Gold embroidered Mogen David (Star of David) and dreidels are beautifully positioned down the length of a navy runner. Gold dishes sit on round, navy blue beaded chargers with gold menorahs around the edges. Gold painted martini glasses enhance the gold of the dishes. A personalized dreidel sits on top of each setting as a place card. A specially designed menorah and a snow globe with a dreidel inside, adding a whimsical touch, are placed at the center of the table.

My Chanukah cupcake design will make everyone smile! A treat to look at as well as to eat, easy to serve and hard to forget.

Involving the Children

Chanukah calls for eight great nights of gift-giving. Homemade cookies are gifts you can make with your children. Bake sugar cookies in the shape of menorahs and dreidels and put them in a nice gift box. With older children, you can make colorful candles and add the name of the guest to the candle or place small trinkets in the hot candle wax so as it burns little gifts are revealed. Each child can make their own menorah using a readily available air hardening modeling clay (DAS by Prang). Mimicking the menorah, they can make groups of nine flowers or footballs or puppies or whatever their minds can conjure up. Have them insert a candle into the soft dough to turn it into a candleholder. After the clay is dry and painted, simply glue the pieces to a small flat piece of wood. Voila! A unique menorah has been created that your child can proudly proclaim as their own!

Caprese Salad

(Dairy) Serves 4-6

2½ cups red and yellow cherry and grape tomatoes, cut in half

3 tablespoons olive oil

4 tablespoons balsamic vinegar

1 teaspoon sugar

Salt and pepper

15 fresh marinated baby mozzarella balls

Fresh basil

Pesto:

3 cups fresh basil

¼ cup toasted pine nuts

¼ cup toasted cashews, unsalted

2 small garlic cloves, peeled and minced

½ cup grated Parmesan cheese

½ cup olive oil

Salt and pepper

For pesto, using a food processor, combine basil, pine nuts, cashews, garlic and Parmesan cheese. Drizzle oil slowly into food processor while it is running; also season with salt and pepper to taste. Pour a small amount of extra olive oil on top of the pesto to keep it from oxidizing and turning brown. Set aside.

Place tomatoes into large bowl. Toss with oil, balsamic vinegar, sugar and salt and pepper to taste. Add mozzarella balls and continue to toss. Let sit a few minutes to absorb flavors. Drain extra oil from pesto and drizzle a small amount over tomatoes and mozzarella balls. Transfer salad to serving dish and add fresh basil to garnish. Serve remaining pesto on the side with baguette slices brushed with olive oil.

Traditional Potato or Vegetable Latkes

(Pareve) *Serves 4-6*

Potato Latkes:

5 potatoes, peeled, grated and squeezed dry

2 small yellow onions, finely chopped

⅔ cup all-purpose flour

1 tablespoon corn starch

2 eggs, lightly beaten

2 teaspoons fresh lemon juice

¼ cup parsley, chopped

¼ cup cilantro, chopped

Salt and pepper

Vegetable oil

Vegetable Latkes:

3 potatoes, peeled, grated and squeezed dry

1 small yellow onion, finely chopped

2 carrots, grated and squeezed dry

2 zucchini, grated and squeezed dry

1 teaspoon turmeric

½ teaspoon ground cumin

¼ sweet paprika

Salt and pepper

Vegetable oil

For potato or vegetable latkes, mix all ingredients together, potatoes through salt and pepper to taste. In a heavy skillet over medium heat, bring ¼-inch of oil to 350°F. Using a measuring cup, scoop 4-5 ¼-cup mounds of latke mixture into skillet. Flatten with a fork to form 3-inch pancakes. Fry on each side 3-4 minutes, until golden brown. Transfer to a baking sheet lined with a paper towel and keep warm in oven (200°F.) while making more latkes.

Blessed are You, LORD our God, King of the universe,
who has granted us life, sustained us, and enabled us
to reach this occasion.

Blooming Chanukiah

Table Description

Chanukiah come in all sizes and shapes, and every family has favorites that are handed down through the generations. Children love making their own using clay and their imaginations. In this table setting, the chanukiah is formed by a series of vases with special lighted bases and filled with cobalt blue colored water. The tall vase in the middle represents the shamash (helper). Creativity is key to keeping the celebration fresh. Here, the prim white daisies coordinate with the navy and silver of the table linens. (Note: Coloring water that will be used with cut flowers should be done at the last minute so the flowers do not unexpectedly change colors!)

Asian Latkes with Sesame Dipping Sauce

(Pareve) Serves 4-6

2 medium potatoes, peeled, grated and squeezed dry

½ cup carrots, grated and squeezed dry

3 scallions, finely chopped

1½ tablespoons cornstarch

1 teaspoon salt

1 egg, slightly beaten

2 tablespoons all-purpose flour

Vegetable oil

Sesame Dipping Sauce:

1 teaspoon sesame seeds

1 small garlic clove, peeled and minced

1 scallion, finely chopped

6 tablespoons soy sauce

¼ cup white vinegar

2 teaspoons sesame oil

2 teaspoons sugar

In a medium bowl, mix together potatoes, carrots and scallions. In a separate small bowl, add cornstarch and salt to egg and mix well. Add egg mixture to potato-carrot mixture. Add flour and mix until incorporated. In a heavy skillet over medium heat, bring ¼-inch of oil to 350°F. Using a measuring cup, scoop 4-5 ¼-cup mounds of latke mixture into skillet. Flatten with a fork to form 3-inch pancakes. Fry on each side 3-4 minutes, until golden brown. Transfer to a baking sheet lined with a paper towel and keep warm in oven (200°F.) while making more latkes.

While latkes are frying, make the dipping sauce by combining all ingredients in a small bowl. Stir until well blended. Serve on the side.

Shimmering Iridescence

Candle lighting was an important part of worship, both in Jewish homes and in the Temple. On this holiday, using a nine-branched chanukiah, unlike the more common seven-branched menorah, families light a candle for each of the eight nights of the holiday to represent the strength of God. The ninth candle in the center of the chanukiah is the "helper" candle, the shamash, used to light the others, starting with the candle on the right. One candle is lit the first night, and each night one additional candle is lit until all nine are glowing. A total of 44 candles are needed to fulfill the lighting ceremonies night by night. It is traditional to let the candles go out on their own, without being extinguished, except on Shabbat. One chanukiah is usually lit for the entire family, though sometimes children like to have their own to light during the holiday.

Typically, three blessings are recited when lighting the candles. On the first night of Chanukah, Jews recite all three blessings; on all subsequent nights, they recite only the first two. The blessings are said before or after the candles are lit depending on tradition. It is customary today to place the chanukiah on the windowsill or near a window. Both options are fine since the most important thing is that passersby are able to see the lit chanukiah and be reminded of the Chanukah miracle.

Table Description

Turquoise, aqua, blue and shimmering iridescent green bring your guests instantly into the night's celebration of Chanukah. It's time to light candles, open gifts and eat the anticipated traditional foods. A white tablecloth is overlaid with a silver runner scattered with blue and silver pebbles and stars. Three matching tall vases make the centerpiece. The two outside vases are filled with silver and aqua balls and the center vase holds blue and white dreidels which anchor a bouquet of peacock feathers. Each place setting starts with a navy blue napkin draped under a green and blue iridescent ruffled charger. A glittering silver plate is placed on the charger and a small favor is wrapped in Mogen David gift wrap with sheer blue ribbons. Matching turquoise iridescent glasses finish the setting. A specially designed chanukiah beautifully completes the table.

Fried Corn Cakes with Sweet Chili Sauce

(Dairy) Serves 4-6

2 cups frozen corn kernels, thawed and drained

3 tablespoons fresh dill, finely chopped

4 scallions, finely chopped

¼ cup red bell pepper, seeds removed and chopped

1 small fresh red chili, seeds removed and finely chopped
   or ½ teaspoon, or less, crushed red pepper

2 eggs

1 cup cheddar cheese, shredded

Salt and white pepper

1 cup flour or corn meal

4 tablespoons water, as needed

Vegetable oil

Mix together corn through cheese. Add salt and pepper to taste. Add flour or corn meal and mix well. If batter is too dry, add water one tablespoon at a time until slightly moistened. Let stand 10-15 minutes.

In a large frying pan over medium-high heat, bring oil to 350°F. Using a measuring cup, scoop 4-5 ¼-cup mounds of batter into skillet. Fry on each side 1½-2 minutes, until golden brown. Transfer to a baking sheet lined with a paper towel and keep warm in oven (200°F.) while making more corn cakes. Serve hot with chili sauce on the side.

Dreidel Fun

Dreidels are important every night of the eight-day celebration, and whether we sing about them, make them out of clay, or simply spin them for a game of put-and-take, the huge variety of colors, sizes and shapes can add cheer to the table. Wherever there are dreidels, can gelt be far away? Mugs brimming with the gold-wrapped chocolate pieces assure everyone that there is plenty to play with, as well as to nosh on.

Table Description

White placemats match the white napkins that are tied with a "Happy Hanukkah" ribbon. Turquoise chargers support white plates decorated with dreidels. At the right of each plate stand cobalt blue glasses that demand your attention. The centerpiece is made up of three vases containing silver branches with dreidels attached to the branches in the tallest vase. Bags of gelt are for the winners of rounds of dreidel and a traditional silver chanukiah finishes the display.

Cream of Broccoli and Mushroom Soup

(Dairy) Serves 4-6

1 stick butter, unsalted

2 leeks, sliced (only use white and light green parts)

2 shallots, minced

3 garlic cloves, peeled and minced

2½ cups broccoli florets

2 cups button mushrooms, sliced

6 cups vegetable broth

Salt and pepper

1 pint heavy cream

½ cup Gruyere, shredded

½ cup Mozzarella, shredded

Melt butter in a heavy bottomed stock pot. Add leeks and shallots, cooking until translucent. Add garlic, broccoli and mushrooms and cook for 4 minutes, stirring constantly. Add vegetable broth and simmer for 25 minutes. Cool slightly and then blend using food processor. Return blended soup to pot and reheat. Season with salt and pepper to taste. Add cream and simmer 10 minutes. Just before serving, place a mix of cheeses in individual soup or bread bowls and then ladle soup on top of cheese.

Baked Cod with Tropical Fruit Relish

(Pareve) Serves 4-6

6 fillets of cod or hake,
  skinless and boneless

2 tablespoons lemon juice

2 tablespoons olive oil

1 teaspoon garlic salt

Ground pepper

Chives

Fruit Relish:

1 cup fresh mango, diced

1 cup fresh papaya, diced

⅓ cup red bell pepper, diced

¼ cup green bell pepper, diced

1 tablespoon green onion, minced

1 tablespoon red jalapeno, minced

2 tablespoons fresh lime juice

1 tablespoon honey

Prepare fruit relish by combining all ingredients in a bowl. Mix well and let sit at room temperature 15-20 minutes.

Preheat oven to 400°F. Brush lemon juice on both sides of fillet and let it rest for 1 minute. Brush both sides of fillet with olive oil and then season both sides with garlic salt and pepper to taste. Bake in oven 5-6 minutes on each side, until fillet flakes easily with a fork. Garnish with chives and serve with fruit relish.

Mogen David

Table Description

A sparkley blue tablecloth makes this table festive enough for the children while still being elegant for the adults. Hand painted goblets with Mogen David patterns are eyecatching, and if made of acrylic, sufficiently durable for the children to use. A simple white napkin is rolled and wrapped with a menorah napkin ring.

Chanukah plates can be handed down to your children, but if you can't find china, a good party store should have fun Chanukah paper plates to add a festive touch to your table. Bring out all of your dreidels so everyone can play. And don't forget the chanukiah to finish out your table.

119

Traditional Sufganyiot

(Dairy) Serves 4-6

4 cups all-purpose flour

1 package dry yeast

⅓ cup sugar

1 cup milk or water

4 eggs, beaten

1 tablespoon brandy

1 tablespoon salt

¼ stick butter

Vegetable oil for deep frying

Jams, jellies, Nutella, whipped cream

Powdered sugar

Mix flour, yeast, sugar and milk (or water) in a mixer with a dough hook. Add eggs, brandy and salt. Knead dough for 7 minutes using a slow to moderate speed. Gradually add butter while continuing to knead until dough is smooth and uniform, without lumps. Remove dough and wrap it in floured plastic wrap. Set aside for 1½ hours at room temperature until doubled in volume. Press down on dough to remove any air, cover again with floured plastic wrap, and refrigerate for 2 hours. Shape dough into small balls. Let rise at room temperature until doubled in volume.

In a large frying pan, heat oil on medium-low heat to 375°F. Fry dough until a "shell" is formed after about 3 minutes. Turn and cook for 3 more minutes. Transfer balls to paper towels to remove excess oil. When cool, using a baker's syringe, or by making a small opening in the dough using a small bread knife, fill with jam, jellies, Nutella or whipped cream. Dust with powdered sugar and serve hot.

Sfenge

(Pareve) Serves 4-6

4 cups all-purpose flour

1 tablespoon salt

3 tablespoons sugar

1 package dry yeast

4 cups water

Vegetable oil for deep frying

Powdered sugar

In a large bowl, mix together flour, salt, sugar and yeast. Add water and mix until batter is smooth. Cover bowl with plastic wrap and kitchen towel. Let sit for 1½ hours in a warm place, until doubled in volume. Shape dough into round balls, and press your finger through to make a doughnut hole.

In a large frying pan, heat oil on medium-low heat to 375°F. When the oil is hot, using a slotted spoon, carefully lower doughnuts into oil, turning them over and over until golden brown. Dust with powdered sugar and serve hot.

Chanukah, Festival of Lights and Warmth

During Chanukah, the children are given gelt (festive chocolate coins wrapped in foil) and real money. Gifts of money present an opportunity to teach children about charity (Tzedakah) and helping those less fortunate. To add more spirit to this festive holiday, collect items from visiting family and friends to give to local charities. Creating a songbook with Chanukah songs in it will allow your guests to celebrate the festival of lights with a sing-along around the dinner table. These songs can easily be found on the internet and, once printed, children can decorate the covers of the songbooks with Chanukah stickers or drawings. Playing the dreidel game is a must, so be sure to stock up on gelt and dreidels, enough for everyone to get involved.

Table Description

Eye-catching flame napkins match the mood of candle lighting for this fun dinner party. Gold chargers make the dinner party feel like a special occasion, while the smaller dinner plates emphasize the intimacy of the gathering. The table is spread with plenty of gelt. Time for good food and fun! Blazing yellow mums or a profusion of flame-colored roses intermingle with small glass vases filled with bright yellow orange juice. When the décor sets the heart to racing, everyone reboots to party mode, ready to laugh and enjoy one another's company.

The Miracle of Children

Chanukah is celebrated in an environment of miracles with a cheerful and tasty chanukiah cake. Frosting candles are bright colors, and the menorah base is made with lots of yummy candies. The cake, served on a festival plate with a chanukiah design, is surrounded by chocolate coins and tiny dreidels. The napkin ring is a flexible flashlight, reminding us that the light dispels the darkness.

Buffet

Table Description

Yes, Chanukah colors usually reflect bright blue, shiny silver, and regal gold, but it is also a time for warm colors that match the candles burning in your cozy home setting. With so many traditional foods to choose from, it can be fun to add the variety of a Chanukah buffet to your nightly celebrations. Shiny gold napkins are rolled tall like a candle flame in the wine glasses. The red, orange and yellow flowers complement the plaid tablecloth, and the bright square platters with a design of houses are stacked and standing ready for the guests. A tall earthenware jug makes a great dispenser for penlights or other gifts children love.

A Chanukah buffet can be anything from a light meal with lots of traditional treats, to a full spread on your table with lots of seating around your fireplace and living areas. Whatever designs you choose, a warm buffet allows you unlimited color selection; but for the best result, pick three to four bright colors to accomplish the effect you want. Enjoy!

Tu B'Shevat

But as for me, I am like a leafy olive tree in the house of God; I trust in the mercy of God for ever and ever.

—PSALM 52:10

Tu B'Shevat was the start of the year when the tithes for the first fruits of the trees were brought to the Temple. Even though the Temple no longer stands, the holiday is still celebrated, with the emphasis being on first fruits, but also on planting trees in Israel. In fact, the holiday is often referred to as the Jewish Arbor Day, or New Year for the tree.

Tu B'Shevat has become an occasion for trees to be planted in Israel, re-foresting a land that was once filled with trees before the destruction of the Second Temple. The Jewish National Fund began by planting eucalyptus trees in the swampy areas of Israel to help end the malaria epidemics. The notion of Tu B'Shevat as a Jewish Arbor Day means that the holiday is often celebrated by planting trees as an act of Tikun Olam (repairing or healing the world).

Trees are symbolic of the Jewish people. The seed is planted deep in the ground and nurtured with water and sunlight. For Jews, the seed is our soul and it is nurtured with Torah study and family. Just like a tree, our strength comes from our roots and those roots are our beliefs.

Table of Life

Table Description

A jute tablecloth is overlaid with olive branch fabric. Stoneware dishes painted with olives sit at each place with a small olive branch on top of the plate. Olive branch fabric makes unique matching napkins. Fill a ceramic urn with olive branches and fresh olives. Remember, fresh olives are not to be eaten before they are cured. Golden wine glasses pick up the golden tones of the urn that makes the centerpiece for this table. Bottles of cured olives wrapped with jute and tied with raffia can be used as place cards and also as a gift for your guests.

The tree has always been a metaphor for Jewish life. The Torah says, "Man is a tree of the field." We are nurtured by deep roots, as far back as Abraham and Sarah. We reach upwards to the heavens while standing firmly on the ground. And when we do all this right, we produce fruits that benefit the world, our good deeds.

Tree imagery is often associated with learning. In synagogue we sing from Proverbs about the Torah, "A tree of life to those that hold fast to her." In the Talmud, those who study or teach Torah are described as trees. And our greatest teachers, our parents, are described as trees with the familiar saying, "The apple doesn't fall far from the tree."

*P**lanting a tree in Israel every year is an important tradition to pass on to your children. Bring your family's attention to the Jewish National Fund Blue Box by having children place money in it sometime during the festive meal.*

Involving the Children

Show your children how to decorate small terracotta flowerpots with tempera paints and glitter. Fill each pot with a seed packet with the guest's name written on it. This is not only a great outdoor activity, but it makes for easier cleanup. Set up a work station for the kids, covered with a throw-away plastic flower-themed table cover. If the children are older, provide supplies for planting a few seeds in medium-size containers. You'll need some potting soil and a gardening scoop, plus a few seed packets.

Warm Goat Cheese and Pomegranate Salad

(Dairy) Serves 4-6

1 log goat cheese, cut into ¾″ rounds

1 egg, beaten

1 cup Panko bread crumbs

3 tablespoons butter

¼ cup olive oil

2 Romaine hearts, washed and chopped into 1″ pieces (reserving a few whole leaves)

¾ cup pomegranate seeds

4 tablespoons pine nuts, toasted

Vinaigrette:

1 teaspoon lemon juice

2 tablespoons balsamic vinegar

1 teaspoon Dijon mustard

1 garlic clove, peeled and minced

¼ cup olive oil

1 teaspoon sugar

Salt and ground pepper

Vinaigrette:

Place all ingredients into a container with a lid. Shake well, until thoroughly mixed together. Place in refrigerator until ready to serve.

Dip goat cheese rounds in egg, then coat with bread crumbs. Heat butter and oil in skillet. Place goat cheese in skillet and fry on each side until golden brown. Transfer goat cheese to paper towels to remove excess oil.

Place whole Romaine leaves on a large platter and top with chopped leaves. Place fried goat cheese rounds on top of salad. Sprinkle with pomegranate seeds and pine nuts. Just before serving vinaigrette, shake once. Serve on the side in a spouted dish.

Miso Marinated Salmon

(Pareve) Serves 4

4 salmon fillets (6-8 ounces each)

1 tablespoon olive oil

1 teaspoon sesame oil

1 garlic clove, peeled and minced

4 ounces shitake mushrooms,
stemmed and sliced

1 large bok choy,
cut crosswise into 1" strips

Salt and pepper

Basmati or jasmine rice, cooked

Marinade:

2 garlic cloves, peeled and minced

⅓ cup green onions, chopped

¼ cup soy sauce

1 tablespoon rice wine or dry sherry

2 teaspoons light brown sugar

1 teaspoon toasted sesame oil

2 tablespoons white miso paste

1 tablespoon ginger, peeled and sliced

Marinade:

Using a food processor or blender, combine all ingredients. In a glass baking dish, arrange salmon and coat with marinade. Marinate in refrigerator for an hour, but no less than 15 minutes.

Preheat oven to 400°F.

Remove salmon from marinade and place on a baking sheet. Bake for about 8 minutes, or until it flakes easily with a fork.

Heat olive oil and sesame oil in a large pan over high heat. Add garlic and mushrooms. Sauté for 3-5 minutes, stirring often until mushrooms are tender. Add bok choy and cook an additional 3 minutes or until leaves are wilted but still green and stalks are still white. Add salt and pepper to taste. Place salmon on top of Gnocci with Sundried Tomatoes (see page 138).

Rustic Harvest Table

A land of wheat and barley, and vines and fig-trees and pomegranates; a land of olive-trees and honey.

—DEUTERONOMY 8:8

Table Description

This table celebrates the new year of the tree by capturing the feeling of farm life. The center of the table has a metal milk jug filled with fresh flowers. It is surrounded by cups of dried fruits, a vase filled with fresh fruits, including clusters of grapes, and a small metal flowerpot filled with daisies. Woven straw chargers in earth tones, with stoneware dishes in complementary colors, pair nicely with a rainbow of colored martini glasses. Napkins are tied with raffia and labeled packets of dried fruits and nuts at each place setting are used as place cards.

Gnocchi with Sun-dried Tomatoes

(Pareve) Serves 4

3 tablespoons olive oil

1 pound fresh potato gnocchi

1 stick butter

1 tablespoon fresh thyme

3 tablespoons fresh parsley, chopped

¼ cup roasted macadamia nuts and walnuts

½ cup sun-dried tomatoes, sliced

Preheat broiler to high.

Heat oil in a large pan until very hot. Add gnocchi and cook gently until golden brown. Transfer gnocchi to paper towels to remove excess oil and set aside.

Heat butter in a large pan. Add thyme and parsley and sauté for 1 minute. Add gnocchi, macadamia nuts and walnuts, tossing to heat through. Serve gnocchi topped with sun-dried tomatoes and Miso Marinated Salmon (see page 135).

Outdoor Fruit Festival

Tu B'Shevat falls at the beginning of spring in Israel, when the winter rains subside and the pink and white blossoms of the almond trees begin to bud. It is for this reason that almonds and other fruits and nuts native to the Land of Israel (barley, dates, figs, grapes, pomegranates, olives, and wheat) are commonly eaten during the Tu B'Shevat meal.

Table Description

This is a simple table with a focus on fruits and flowers. White flower chargers hold floral print dishes. Green napkins are tied with artificial flowers as napkin rings and floral mugs duplicate the table decorations. A white metal bicycle cart holds apples and oranges, and a large platter displays nuts and dried fruits, as well as grapes and fresh strawberries for nibbling. An enameled water jug holds flowering almond tree branches arching gracefully over the table. A metal flower pot is filled with cabbage roses and peonies, and delicate silk butterflies complete the look of springtime.

Butternut Squash and Sweet Potato Bisque

(Dairy) Serves 4-6

1 medium yellow onion, diced

1 tablespoon butter

1 tablespoon curry powder

3 cups vegetable stock

2 cups butternut squash, peeled and chopped

1 cup sweet potato, peeled and chopped

1 apple, peeled, cored and chopped

½ cup heavy cream

Salt and pepper

Pumpkin seeds, toasted

In a stockpot, sauté onions in butter until soft. Add curry powder, vegetable stock, butternut squash, sweet potato and apple. Bring to a boil and cook 30 minutes or until vegetables are soft. Using a blender or food processor, blend until smooth. Return to stockpot, add cream and heat through. Season with salt and pepper to taste. Serve with a garnish of pumpkin seeds.

Lemon Mélange

When thou shalt besiege a city a long time, in making war against it to take it, thou shalt not destroy the trees thereof by wielding an axe against them; for thou mayest eat of them, but thou shalt not cut them down; for is the tree of the field man, that it should be besieged of thee?

—DEUTERONOMY 20:19

Table Description

Crisp white and yellow striped bar towels with a lemon print become placemats for this bright and sunny table. Square plates with painted lemons and matching square bowls top the placemats. The bowls have kumquats for nibbling and a carafe of lemonade is ready to be poured into green wine glasses. In lieu of a typical flower arrangement, a lemon arrangement sits on the table while a carafe filled with lemon slices and tulips mirrors the carafe of lemonade. A platter with lemon cake is ready to be served for dessert.

Lovely Lemons

Table Description

This outdoor Tu B'Shevat table celebrates the sweetness of the lemon blossom and the beauty of bright yellow lemons. A green striped runner presents the table with lemon candle holders and a basket of lemons. A tall woven basket is filled with branches from a lemon tree, including the fragrant lemon blossoms which will entice the senses. Large square green plates are used as chargers and smaller square plates with painted lemons are placed on top. A printed lemon napkin is simply folded and green and yellow handled silverware repeat the tones of the lemons. Green stoneware mugs complete the table and can be filled with a lemon and mint tea to finish off a lovely meal.

The First Fruits

*"Did I shelter the seedlings
that live in my shade—so
they will grow up to be a
next generation like myself?"*

—"A TREE'S NEW YEAR'S RESOLUTION"
BY SHLOMO YAFFE

Table Description

*In the spirit of gratitude to God for the first fruits
of the field, this table is set with varieties of
citrus. Cover a round table with a simple yellow
tablecloth to bring out the colors of the limes,
lemons, kumquats and oranges placed in a tall
cylinder for a centerpiece. Plates designed as
orange slices are used to reflect the warm sunny
days of spring, and green napkins are folded to
look like leaves. Asymmetrical orange glass vases
are placed on either side of the centerpiece, and
branches from an orange tree are placed on the
table. Glasses with a lemon print are filled with
ice cold lemonade and a lemon cake completes
the warm citrus table. Guests should feel free
to grab an orange or Clementine from the table
at the end of the meal and to nibble on the
kumquats at their place setting.*

And when
ye shall come
into the land,
and shall
have
planted all
manner of trees
for food.

—LEVITICUS 19:23

Jewish National Fund

Based on the proposal of a German Jewish mathematician, Zvi Hermann Schapira, the Jewish National Fund (JNF), with Theodor Herzl's support, was founded at the Fifth Zionist Congress in Basel in 1901. For more than 100 years, JNF has evolved into a global environmental leader by planting more than 250 million trees, building over 240 reservoirs and dams, developing over 250,000 acres of land, creating more than 2,000 parks, providing the infrastructure for over 1,000 communities, and connecting thousands of children and young adults to Israel and their heritage.

The Blue Box has been part of the JNF since its inception, symbolizing the partnership between Israel and the Diaspora. In the period between the two World Wars, about one million of these blue and white tin collection boxes could be found in Jewish homes throughout the world. The funds raised through the Blue Box (the "pushke," as it was widely known) were an instrument to redeeming the land in Eretz Israel on which the Jewish home was to arise. But the Blue Box was more than just a fundraising device. From the beginning, it was an important educational vehicle spreading the Zionist word and forging the bond between the Jewish people and their ancient homeland.

In 2002, the JNF was awarded the Israel Prize for lifetime achievement and special contribution to society and the State of Israel.

Planting trees is a big part of Tu B'Shevat, but so is the idea of healing the world. Put together a selection of small plants, and a tray full of fresh and dried fruits, as gifts for your guests. Plan to make extras to deliver to a local nursing home, or to a friend or family member who could use the encouraging gift. You will be pleased to see how passing along a little kindness can brighten the paths of others.

As with the Passover seder, the Tu B'Shevat seder evolved to include four cups of wine which represent the seasons: white for the bleak time of winter, white with a bit of red for the earth's awakening in early spring, red with a bit of white representing the blossoming of late spring, and dark red to represent the fullness of all the growing plants and vegetation in the heat of summer.

With the rise of Zionism in the late 19th century, Tu B'Shevat was rediscovered as a celebration that links the Jews with their land. The holiday became one of rededication to the ecology of the denuded land, with the planting of trees taking center stage in the celebration. Jews outside of Israel contribute money to plant trees there and/or plant trees in their own communities.

My Roots

Table Description

A blanket in the forest with pillows and small stools make a comfortable resting place in the shade. Welcome your guests with fresh and dried fruit in a clay pot. A special milk bottle holds the beverage. Place the plates on clay pot saucers as the chargers, and use a small clay pot as the napkin ring. And don't forget to place the JNF Blue Box as the centerpiece.

Crème Brulée

(Dairy) Serves 6

9 egg yolks

¾ cup superfine sugar, plus 6 tablespoons

3 cups heavy cream

I vanilla bean

Preheat oven to 325°F. Using a whisk in a large bowl, cream together egg yolks and ¾ cup sugar until mixture is thick and pale yellow. Set aside.

Pour cream into a medium saucepan over low heat. Using a paring knife, split vanilla bean down the middle, scrape out the seeds and add seeds to the cream. Bring cream to a brief simmer, without allowing it to boil. Remove cream from heat.

Temper the egg yolks by gradually whisking the cream into the yolk and sugar mixture, stirring constantly to prevent the eggs from scrambling.

Divide the custard into six 6-ounce ramekins (ceramic bowls), about three quarters full. Place ramekins in a roasting pan and fill pan with enough hot water to come halfway up the sides of the ramekins. Bake until barely set around the edges, about 40 minutes. Remove from oven and cool to room temperature.

Chill in refrigerator for 2 hours.

Sprinkle I tablespoon sugar on top of each chilled custard. Hold a kitchen torch 2 inches above the surface to melt the sugar and form a crust (or you may place under broiler until sugar melts, about 2 minutes).

Zucchini Nut Chocolate Cake

(Dairy) Serves 8-10

2¼ cups all-purpose flour

½ cup unsweetened cocoa

1 teaspoon baking soda

1 teaspoon salt

1¾ cups sugar

½ cup butter, softened

½ cup canola oil

2 large eggs

1 teaspoon vanilla extract

½ cup buttermilk

2 cups zucchini, grated

1 cup almonds, finely chopped

Powdered sugar

Raspberry sauce

Preheat oven to 325°F. Sift together flour, cocoa, baking soda and salt. Set aside. In a medium bowl mix together sugar, butter and oil. When creamed thoroughly, add eggs, one at a time, vanilla extract, buttermilk, zucchini and almonds. Continue stirring until fully incorporated.

Slowly add flour mixture to batter. When thoroughly mixed together, pour batter into a greased and floured 9″ x 13″ baking dish. Bake 50 minutes, until a cake tester comes out clean from the center. If desired, dust with powdered sugar before serving. Zigzag raspberry sauce onto dessert plates. Place each serving of cake on top of raspberry sauce. Top servings with fresh raspberries or other seasonal fruit.

Purim

Purim

Now in the twelfth month,
which is the month Adar, on
the thirteenth day of the same,
...in the day that the enemies
of the Jews hoped to have
rule over them; whereas it was
turned to the contrary, that the
Jews had rule over them that
hated them.

—ESTHER 9:1

Purim is one of the most happy and joyful holidays on the Jewish calendar. It commemorates a time when the Jewish people living in Persia were saved from extermination. Purim means "lots." The name commemorates the lots that Haman cast to choose the day most suitable for the destruction of the Jews. The 13th of Adar is the day that Haman chose, and the day the Jews battled their enemies for their lives. On the following day, the 14th, they celebrated their survival.

In cities that were protected by a surrounding wall at the time of Joshua, Purim is instead celebrated on the 15th of the month on what is known as Shushan Purim. Today, only Jerusalem celebrates Purim on the 15th. In leap years, when there are two months of Adar, Purim is celebrated in the second month of Adar, so it is always one month before Passover.

Pretty in Pink

Table Description

The pink table setting sparkles with even more whimsical colors, textures and party pizzaz. Feathers turn ordinary plates into a showcase for gift-giving when used as a charger trim. A colorful carton holds the wine to be served in flower-print wine glasses.

Purim is a community holiday of joyful celebration. The centerpiece of the communal celebration is the reading of the Scroll of Esther in the synagogue. According to the Book of Esther in the Hebrew Bible, Haman, royal vizier to King Ahasuerus, planned to kill all the Jews in the empire on the 13th of Adar. However, his plans were blocked by Mordecai and his adopted daughter, Queen Esther.

It is customary to boo, make lots of noise, stamp feet and rattle graggers (noisemakers) whenever the name of Haman is mentioned during the reading of the Book of Esther. The reason for this custom is to blot out the name of this horrible evildoer.

We are commanded to celebrate with a special festive meal called the Purim Se'udah. The drinking of wine features prominently in keeping with the jovial nature of the feast. This is based on the fact that the salvation of the Jews occurred through wine, and the Sages of the Talmud stated that one should drink on Purim until he can no longer distinguish between the phrases *arur Haman* (cursed is Haman) and *baruch Mordechai* (blessed is Mordecai).

The overriding theme of Purim is the saving of the Jews from a mortal threat. Even though God is not mentioned at all in the Book of Esther, from a Jewish perspective God is the one who is pulling the strings of redemption behind the scenes. Within this tension between an unseen God and a story seemingly driven by arbitrary fate, a number of other fascinating themes emerge. Mordecai was called upon to write a decree to reverse the command of the King, and the Jews were victorious over their enemies. Esther wrote another decree commanding the days of feasting and giving to the poor to be observed as an annual celebration by all Jewish households.

...and on the fourteenth day of the same they rested, and made it a day of feasting and gladness.

—ESTHER 9:17

The Book of Esther prescribes "sending portions one to another, and gifts of the poor" (9:22). According to halakha, each adult must send food gifts to friends (*mishloach manot*) and make a charitable contribution to the poor (*matanot la'evyonim*). The mitzvah of giving *mishloach manot* derives from the Book of Esther. Sending gifts of food to one another ensures that everyone will have enough for the Purim feast held later in the day. The gift-giving also increases love and friendship among Jews, which runs contrary to Haman's desire to wrongly characterize the Jewish people as lacking harmony and unity of spirit.

On the day of Purim, it is also a special mitzvah to give money to at least two poor people. Each poor person should be given at least the amount of food that is usually eaten at a regular meal, or the amount of money required to buy this. It is preferable to do this after the Megillah reading (the reading of the Book of Esther), so that the blessing "She'hecheyanu" can apply to it. It is better to spend more on gifts to the poor than on gifts to friends. There is no greater joy than gladdening the hearts of orphans, widows and the poor. The Jewish people are one unit—we can't possibly enjoy the holiday if less fortunate people don't have enough.

...to enjoin them that they should keep the fourteenth day of the month Adar, and the fifteenth day of the same, yearly, the days wherein the Jews had rest from their enemies, and the month which was turned unto them from sorrow to gladness, and from mourning into a good day; that they should make them days of feasting and gladness, and of sending portions one to another, and gifts of the poor.

—ESTHER 9:21-22

Drinks, a festive meal, unique costumes, and fun games make Purim a special party day. Top it off with colorful dishes, including irresistible Hamantaschen. And since you are the Queen today, don't forget to put on your crown!

Involving the Children

It is easy to engage children in the celebration of Purim, enlisting their help ahead of time. The triangular cookies known as Hamantaschen can be prepared in advance, and store-bought crank-style graggers (noisemakers) can be decorated. Or better yet, unique homemade graggers can be made using plastic containers filled with rice and beans, and decorated with stickers, glitter glue, feathers and streamers.

Rainbow Beet and Arugula Salad

(Dairy) Serves 4-6

3 small red beets

3 small golden beets

6 mini sweet bell peppers

1 cup Gorgonzola or goat cheese, crumbled

1 package baby arugula

Dressing:

2 tablespoons honey

2½ tablespoons balsamic vinegar

2½ tablespoons olive oil

Salt

Freshly ground black pepper

Prepare dressing by combining all ingredients until well incorporated. Set aside.

Preheat oven to 350°F. Brush beets lightly with oil. Wrap each beet separately in foil and place on baking sheet in oven. Bake for 45 minutes. Allow beets to cool. Wearing disposable gloves (to prevent stains), peel beets and slice into ¼″ rounds. Set aside.

Preheat broiler to high. Cut off one side of each bell pepper and stuff with crumbled cheese. Place peppers under broiler until cheese is melted and bubbly.

Place a small bunch of arugula in the center of each serving plate. Alternate colored beet slices around the edge of the plate, slightly overlapped. Drizzle dressing over arugula and beets. Place stuffed pepper on top and serve.

Joyful Purim

Table Description

Polka dot ceramic plates and mugs carry the clown theme, and feathers, masks and anything with smiles adds to it. The azure napkins are fastened with elastic beads; candy necklaces could easily be substituted. The centerpiece in this celebration setting can be used in any party setting. It represents a sense of surprise and suspense: "Who is going to get what?" The base is made of a planter with low-lying greens, and the soil acts as a perfect anchor for the tall lollipops. The centerpiece sits atop a box filled with Purim gifts, such as wine, candy and Hamantaschen.

Butternut Squash Ravioli
with Brown Butter Pomodoro Sauce

(Dairy) Serves 4-6

Filling:

5 cups butternut squash, peeled and cubed

2 tablespoons sea salt

1¾ cup freshly grated Parmesan cheese

⅔ cup walnuts, toasted and chopped

¼ teaspoon nutmeg

Salt and pepper

Preheat oven to 350°F. Place squash in greased baking dish and sprinkle liberally with salt. Bake 30-45 minutes, until tender. Puree squash until smooth. Add 1 cup Parmesan cheese, walnuts, nutmeg and a pinch of salt and pepper. Set aside.

Sauce:

28-ounce can of whole peeled tomatoes, with juice

2½ tablespoons olive oil

½ medium onion, diced

2 garlic cloves, peeled and minced

1½ tablespoons fresh oregano, chopped

8 fresh basil leaves, torn in small pieces

½ teaspoon sugar

¼ teaspoon sea salt

¼ teaspoon fresh ground black pepper

Pour tomatoes with juice into a large bowl and crush tomatoes into small chunks. Set aside. Heat olive oil over medium-high heat in a large pan. Add onion and garlic, cooking until onion is tender and translucent. Add tomatoes, oregano, basil, sugar, salt and pepper. Bring to a boil. Reduce heat to a simmer and cook uncovered for 35 minutes.

Pasta:

2¼ cups all-purpose flour

½ teaspoon sea salt

2 large eggs at room temperature

1 teaspoon olive oil

Pasta maker

1 large egg, beaten with
  1 tablespoon water

Garnish:

3 tablespoons unsalted butter

Salt

½ cup freshly grated Parmesan cheese

¼ cup fresh parsley, finely chopped

Pasta:

In a large shallow bowl, shape flour and salt into a mound and create a well in the center. Add eggs and oil into the well. Using a fork, gradually beat the ingredients together, slowly adding more and more of the flour. Mix with fork until dough is a dry, crumbly mixture. Transfer dough to a lightly flour-covered surface and knead 3-5 minutes by hand until all the flour is incorporated and the dough begins to soften and is no longer sticky. Shape dough into a ball, cover with plastic wrap and kitchen towel and let sit for 30 minutes.

Adjust pasta maker to its widest setting, then cut the dough into two portions, shaping each into a flat disk. Flatten one edge of the disk until it fits between the rollers. Feed dough into the rollers and start rolling out the dough, stretching the dough as it feeds through. Sprinkle lightly with flour, fold into thirds, and roll it through again. Repeat 12-14 times, folding into half each time before rolling the dough out. Adjust pasta maker to next setting, fold dough in half and roll out once. Repeat on the middle setting, and dust with flour. Roll out the dough on the next to last setting to form a sheet the same width as the pasta maker, 24 inches long and 1/8″ thick. Repeat these steps with the second piece of dough.

Brush each 24″ sheet of pasta with egg wash. Cut into 4″ squares and place a tablespoon of filling in the center of each square. Bring all edges up to the top and squeeze the upper edges together to form a purse. Transfer to a lightly flour-covered surface.

Heat 1-2 cups of sauce in a large sauté pan over medium heat. In a separate sauté pan melt butter until browned. Add a pinch of salt.

Add the ravioli purses to 5 quarts of boiling salted water and cook for 2-3 minutes. Spoon a small amount of sauce on each plate and add purses. Garnish with Parmesan cheese and chopped parsley. Pour browned butter over the top of each plate and serve immediately.

Rainbow Party

On that day did the king Ahasuerus give the house of Haman the Jews' enemy unto Esther the queen. And Mordecai came before the king; for Esther had told what he was unto her.

—ESTHER 8:1

On Purim there are no particular foods that must be served, though dessert will usually include traditional treats such as Hamantaschen (Haman's pockets), triangular shaped cookies filled with fruit marmalade or sweet poppy seeds. These cookies are intended to represent Haman's three-cornered hat. Others say that they represent Esther's strength and the three founders of Judaism: Abraham, Isaac and Jacob.

It is also customary to eat seeds and nuts on Purim, as the Talmud relates that Queen Esther ate only these foodstuffs in the palace of Ahasuerus, since she had no access to kosher food.

Table Description

Shiny blue silk sets the scene for an explosion of rainbow colors, all mismatched just for fun. The party plates echo various celebration themes, and the striped sateen napkins provide a unifying contrast color. The napkin rings are made from inexpensive jewelry, emphasizing the idea of royalty, because much of the story of Esther unfolds in the King's and Queen's courts. Mismatched flatware accompanies the party plates. A row of tassel-topped foil party hats, surrounded by generous handfuls of chocolate dots, serve as the easy centerpiece.

Hamentaschen with Assorted Fillings

(Dairy) 25 cookies

The tradition to eat Hamantaschen on Purim began in Europe. The word Hamantaschen is derived from two German words: mohn (poppy seed) and taschen (pockets). Mohntaschen is German for "poppy seed pockets" and was a popular German pastry. Hamantaschen means "Haman's pockets" and became a popular Purim pastry. It was rumored that the evil Haman's pockets were filled with bribe money.

3 cups flour, sifted

1 teaspoon baking powder

⅔ cup sugar

¾ cup butter or margarine

½ cup sour cream

2 eggs

1 tablespoon lemon juice

1 teaspoon vanilla extract

2 teaspoons rum extract

1 cup of chocolate, melted

Sprinkles or nuts for garnish

Mix together flour, baking powder and sugar. Add remaining ingredients (butter through rum extract) and mix until fully incorporated. Divide dough into two portions. Cover with plastic wrap and kitchen towel and place in refrigerator for 1 hour.

Preheat oven to 375°F. On a lightly flour-covered surface roll out dough to ⅛" thick. Cut into 3½" circles using a biscuit cutter or an empty glass. Place 1-2 teaspoons of filling into the center of the circle and fold edges over to create a triangle. Pinch the corners tightly so the cookies retain their shape during baking. Space cookies evenly on a greased baking pan. Bake about 18-20 minutes. When cool, dip corners in melted chocolate, then in the sprinkles or nuts.

Fillings: Each of these fillings is enough for the whole batch. If you want to do more than one flavor, reduce the quantities accordingly.

PEANUT BUTTER AND CHOCOLATE CHIP

1 cup peanut butter

½ cup chocolate chips

Mix until well blended.

JAM

1 cup apricot jam or

1 cup raspberry preserves

DATES AND NUTS

½ cup dates, finally chopped

½ cup nuts, finely chopped

Cinnamon to taste

Mix until well blended.

POPPY SEED

1 cup milk

⅔ cup sugar

2 tablespoons honey

1½ cups poppy seeds

2 tablespoons butter, melted

2-3 tablespoons graham cracker crumbs

¼ cup walnuts, finely chopped

⅓ cup raisins

In a small pan, bring milk to low boil and add sugar and honey. Add poppy seeds and continue cooking on low heat for 3-4 minutes, until the seeds absorb the liquid. Remove from heat and add butter. Cool and add graham cracker crumbs, walnuts and raisins.

Gifts and Lollypops

Table Description

Whether putting on a full-scale dinner celebration or hosting an inviting dessert table, this setting is child-friendly as well as simple to arrange. All the treats—noisemakers, candy, cookies, or gifts—are close at hand and touchable. Instead of a tall centerpiece aimed at adults, a mix of candy and gifts is offered in a low-lying plastic hat. Party hats, Hamantaschen, feathers and noisemakers are strewn across the light blue, crinkled tablecloth that places the goodies in "touch and take" mode. Each plate has a feathery mask ready for drama. A few feathers in rainbow colors tucked under each plastic plate boost the fun quotient up just a little bit.

And that these days should be remembered and kept throughout every generation, every family, every province, and every city; and that these days of Purim should not fail from among the Jews, nor the memorial of them perish from their seed.

—ESTHER 9:28

Poppy Seed Cake with White Chocolate

(Dairy) Serves 8-10

⅔ cup butter, softened

2 cups sugar

4 eggs

½ cup poppy seeds

¾ cup sweetened coconut, shredded

Zest of 1 lemon

2 cups all-purpose flour

¾ tablespoon baking powder

2 cups heavy cream

1 cup white chocolate, chopped

Glaze:

1½ cups white chocolate,
    broken into pieces

½ cup of heavy cream

Garnish:

½ cup white chocolate, grated

Preheat oven to 350°F.

Using mixer on medium speed, whip butter with sugar until fluffy, adding eggs
one at a time.

In a separate bowl, mix together poppy seeds, coconut, lemon zest, flour, and baking
powder. Alternately add into the mixing bowl a third of the flour mixture and a third
of the cream, blending together on low speed. Add white chocolate.

Pour mixture into two greased loaf pans. Bake 50 minutes, until a toothpick inserted
in the center comes out with crumbs on it. Remove the cakes from the pans and
cool to room temperature.

Glaze:

Melt chocolate in a double boiler and then add cream. Stir gently and let cool for
a few minutes. Pour the glaze over the cakes, allowing it to drip down the sides.
Garnish with grated chocolate.

Passover

And this day shall be unto you for a
memorial, and ye shall keep it a feast to
the LORD; throughout your generations ye
shall keep it a feast by an ordinance for ever.
Seven days shall ye eat unleavened bread;
howbeit the first day ye shall put away
leaven out of your houses;…And ye shall
observe the feast of unleavened bread;
for in this selfsame day have I brought your
hosts out of the land of Egypt; therefore
shall ye observe this day throughout your
generations by an ordinance for ever.

—EXODUS 12:14-15, 17

The eight-day festival of Passover is celebrated in the early spring,
from the 15th through the 22nd of the Hebrew month of Nisan.
It commemorates the emancipation of the Israelites from slavery
in ancient Egypt. By following the rituals of Passover, we have
the ability to relive and experience the true freedom that our
ancestors gained.

The name "Passover" is derived from the Hebrew word *Pesach*
which is based on the root "pass over." This refers to the fact that
God "passed over" the houses of the Jews when He (through the
Angel of Death) was slaying the firstborn of Egypt during the last
of the ten plagues. In addition, Pesach is the name of the sacrificial
offering (a lamb) that was made in the Temple on this holiday.
Passover is also widely referred to as Hag HaAviv (Spring Festival),
Hag HaMatzot (Festival of Matzah), and Zeman Herutenu
(Time of Our Freedom).

In the narrative of the Exodus, the Bible tells us that God helped the children of Israel escape slavery in Egypt by inflicting ten plagues upon the Egyptians before the Pharaoh would release his Israelite slaves; the tenth and worst of the plagues was the death of the Egyptian firstborn. The Israelites were to mark the doorposts of their homes with the blood of a spring lamb and, upon seeing this, the LORD knew to "pass over" these homes, hence the name of the holiday.

Hag HaMatzot
(FESTIVAL OF MATZAH)

Probably the most significant observance related to Passover involves avoiding chametz (leaven) throughout the Passover holiday. This commemorates the fact that the Jews leaving Egypt were in a hurry, and did not have time to let their bread rise. It is also a symbolic way of removing the "puffiness" (arrogance, pride) from our souls. Interestingly, the loaves of bread offered to God were always unleavened.

Chametz includes anything made from the five major grains (wheat, rye, barley, oats and spelt) that has not been completely cooked within 18 minutes of first coming into contact with water.

On the night before Passover, all chametz is rounded up from the household and a ceremonial burning of the chametz takes place the following morning. Chametz that cannot be disposed of can be sold to a non-Jew for the duration of the holiday.

Passover is a holiday full of ritual symbols that retell the Exodus story. Many of these symbols are displayed on the seder plate, most of which will be eaten before the seder is completed: shankbone of a lamb (representing the paschal sacrifice); burnt hardboiled egg (symbolizing the Jews' strong/hard determination not to abandon their beliefs under Egyptian oppression); bitter herb (representing the bitterness of slavery); charoset (an apple, honey, wine and nut mixture representing the mortar used by the Israelites to build the palaces of Egypt), salt water (slaves' tears), green herb (parsley, or sometimes lettuce, representing new life).

Table Description

The table invites everyone to enthusiastically participate in the Passover seder. Placemats with a matzah print lay under green chargers that hold unique matzah print plates. There are small figures representing some of the ten plagues, in this case locusts, snakes and frogs. The centerpiece is a short vase filled with papyrus branches similar to those used by Yocheved, the mother of Moses, to create the ark that held Moses when he was put into the Nile.

Baby Moses or a frog, it's your choice with these two Passover cupcake designs. Be sure to order cupcakes or use a recipe or mix that is free of leaven and is kosher for Passover.

Involving the Children

Arts and crafts are an important way for the children to connect to the holiday. Each child can draw a piece of matzah on paper or you may prefer to print a matzah graphic. Have the children cut a strip that is 8″ long and 2″ wide. Make a circle from the strip and glue the ends together. You now have a lovely napkin ring that your children can be proud of. You can personalize each napkin ring by writing the name of a guest on it. The children can use the same matzah paper (handmade or printed graphic) to make place cards. All they need to do is cut a square or rectangle from the paper, fold it in half, and write the name of the guest on the outside of the fold.

Bastille–Tripolitania Potato Croquettes with Onion and Mushroom

(Pareve) Makes 6-8 croquettes

6 medium potatoes, peeled, boiled and mashed

4 tablespoons fresh parsley, chopped

2 tablespoons dried dill

1 medium onion, chopped

4 tablespoons canola oil

2 cups mushrooms, stems removed and finely chopped

2 tablespoons mushroom powder

Salt and pepper

2 cups matzah flour

2 large eggs, beaten with 1 tablespoon water

½ cup canola oil

Gently add parsley and dill to mashed potatoes. Season with salt and pepper to taste. Fry onion in oil until golden. Add mushrooms and fry until mixture is blended and brown-gold in color. Add mushroom powder, salt and pepper to taste, and mix together.

Place a large spoonful of mashed potatoes into the palm of your wet hand, forming a patty. Add a spoonful of the onion-mushroom mixture on top of the potato patty. Top the mixture with another potato patty, rounding and sealing the edges to produce a large croquette. Lightly cover croquettes first in flour, then egg wash. Heat oil in large pan and add croquettes, frying until golden, about 2-3 minutes on each side. Remove from pan, blotting with paper towels to absorb excess oil.

Classic Celebration

Table Description

This Passover table celebrates spring in a classic style. Gold, amber and earth tones are brightened with a gorgeous centerpiece of salmon-yellow roses, such as the Fire and Ice variety. Butterflies flutter around the roses. Gold chargers have been placed upon smoky glass placemats and golden-edged ecru napkins, fastened with matzah-patterned rings, complete the effect. A highlight for the table is the manner in which the matzah is displayed. A rectangular vase was found to perfectly display the matzah vertically.

Spicy Hot Moroccan Olive Salad

(Pareve) Serves 4-6

2 cups pitted Manzanilla olives with pimentos

¼ cup canola oil

6 sweet mini peppers, seeds removed and diced

6 garlic cloves, sliced

1 tablespoon sweet paprika

½ tablespoon turmeric

1 tablespoon cumin (optional)

Salt and pepper

3 tablespoons tomato paste

2 large tomatoes, peeled and chopped

¾ cup of water

Place olives in a bowl and rinse with water. Drain and set aside. Heat oil in a sauté pan and add sweet peppers, frying slightly. Stirring gently, add garlic, paprika, turmeric, cumin (optional), and salt and pepper to taste. Add tomato paste and cook, stirring constantly, for about 2 minutes. Add tomatoes and stir for 1 minute. Add olives and water and continue cooking on low heat for 30 minutes. Serve warm or cold.

Roger

Gifts of Gold

Charoset is one of the symbolic foods that Jews eat during the annual Passover seder. A traditional understanding of charoset is that it represents the mortar used by the Israelites to make bricks while they were slaves in Egypt. The word charoset comes from the Hebrew word *cheres*, which means "clay."

As Passover commemorates the Israelites' escape from bondage, a small amount of charoset is placed on the seder plate as a reminder that we were once slaves and are now free. In this way, Passover not only ensures that we remember the past, but it also reminds us to continue to pursue freedom and justice in every generation.

Table Description

The golden hues on this table are intentionally striking. When the Israelites were told to leave Mitzrayim (Egypt), Moses instructed them to go to the Egyptians to ask for gifts; and they were given great treasures (Exodus 12:35-36). The gold-leafed branches, walnuts and wine cups show how the Israelites were rewarded by God. The plates are framed with gold leaf as well, connecting to the golden centerpiece, its tea lights creating a radiant glow.

Chicken Soup with Beef-Filled Matzah Balls

(Meat) 4-6 servings

Chicken Soup:

1 large chicken, washed and quartered

3 large carrots, cut into 1″ slices

3 stalks of celery with leaves, cut into thirds

2 medium onions, quartered

3 quarts cold water

2 bay leaves

8 sprigs fresh parsley, divided

8 sprigs fresh dill, divided

8 sprigs fresh cilantro, divided

2 teaspoons sea salt

2 teaspoons whole peppercorns

Place chicken and vegetables in a large stock pot over medium heat. Add enough water to cover. Add bay leaves, 4 sprigs each of parsley, dill and cilantro, plus salt to taste and peppercorns. Bring slowly to a boil. Lower heat to medium-low and gently simmer for 1½ hours, partially covered, until chicken is done. As the soup cooks, skim any impurities that rise to the surface, adding a little more water, as needed, to keep the chicken covered. Before chicken is cooked through, add remaining parsley and dill.

Matzah Dough:

2 large eggs, slightly beaten

¼ cup hot chicken broth

¼ cup vegetable oil

I cup matzah meal

I tablespoon parsley or dill,
  finely chopped

Salt and freshly ground
  black pepper

Beat eggs lightly into chicken broth, adding oil until eggs and oil are absorbed into the broth. Add remaining ingredients and mix together. The mixture should have the consistency of lightly mashed potatoes. Cover mixture and refrigerate for 3 hours.

Filling:

½ small onion, finely chopped

1½ tablespoons olive or vegetable oil

I pound ground beef, crumbled

I tablespoon fresh parsley, finely chopped

I tablespoon fresh cilantro, finely chopped

2 tablespoons ketchup

¾ tablespoon Worcestershire

¾ tablespoon sweet paprika

½ tablespoon mushroom powder
  (optional)

I tablespoon kosher salt

I teaspoon ground black pepper

In a medium skillet, sauté onion in oil over a medium-high heat until soft. Add beef and continue to sauté. Add remaining ingredients and mix well. Cook until meat is fully brown. Set aside to cool.

Matzah Balls:

With wet hands, shape the matzah dough into balls. Burrow your index finger into the middle of each ball, making a hole. Fill the ball with I teaspoon of the meat filling. Close the hole of the matzah dough and shape into a ball. Keep a small bowl of water nearby to moisten your hands periodically to prevent sticking. Drop the meat-filled matzah balls into the simmering chicken soup and cook for 30 minutes. Garnish bowl of soup and matzah balls with fresh dill and serve.

Spring Butterflies

When thy son asketh thee in time to come, saying:
"What mean the testimonies, and the statutes, and the
ordinances, which the LORD our God hath commanded you?"
then thou shalt say unto thy son: "We were Pharaoh's
bondmen in Egypt; and the LORD brought us out of Egypt
with a mighty hand. And the LORD showed signs and
wonders, great and sore, upon Egypt, upon Pharaoh,
and upon all his house, before our eyes. And He brought us
out from thence, that He might bring us in, to give us
the land which He swore unto our fathers."

—DEUTERONOMY 6:20-23

The text of the Passover seder is written in a book called the Haggadah. The Haggadah tells the story of the Exodus from Egypt and explains some of the practices and symbols of the holiday. The content of the seder can be summed up by the following Hebrew rhyme:

Kaddesh, Urechatz, Karpas, Yachatz, Maggid, Rachtzah, Motzi, Matzah, Maror, Korekh, Shulchan Orekh, Tzafun, Barekh, Hallel, Nirtzah

(Sanctifying the day, washing, green vegetable, breaking the matzah, telling the story, washing and blessing, blessing bread/matzah, blessing for eating matzah, blessing for bitter herbs, charoset-bitter herbs-matzah sandwich, the festive meal, dessert, blessing after meal, psalms, conclusion.)

Table Description

The bright colors of spring burst off the table by having a white tablecloth, spring flowers, flower-themed plates on green chargers, butterflies, and matzah-print napkin rings. The special wine glasses have flower prints joining together the centerpiece, the plates and the overall spring theme.

On This Night We Eat Matzah

Table Description

This Passover table reflects beauty and formality. The dark wooden table is dressed with orange and yellow spring flowers shown in amber colored mosaic cups on metal trivets topped with bronze colored glass. The two centerpieces are offset by the matzah-themed runner and surrounded by stately bronze wine glasses. Spring butterfly plates pay homage to the season. Bronze chargers hold square, white plates with a matzah-print napkin folded like a pocket, where you can place the Haggadah.

Almond Cookies

(Kosher) Makes 15-20 cookies

Four egg yolks

1 cup white sugar

1 pound white almonds, coarsely chopped

1¼ tablespoon almond extract

1 cup good quality dark chocolate, melted

Preheat oven to 350°F. In a bowl, mix together eggs and white sugar. Beat well. Add almonds and vanilla extract and continue mixing together. Drop dough by spoonfuls onto a cookie sheet covered with parchment paper. Bake 12-15 minutes, or until edges are lightly browned.

Remove cookies to cooling rack covered with parchment paper. When cookies are cool, drizzle with melted chocolate.

Passover Brownies

(Pareve) Makes 12-16 brownies

1½ cups dark chocolate

1½ cups margarine, softened

¼ cup sugar

5 whole eggs

6-ounce package instant chocolate pudding (kosher for Passover)

1½ cups walnuts, chopped

1 cup chocolate chips and/or raisins or ½ cup shredded coconut (optional)

Preheat oven to 350°F. In large saucepan, melt chocolate and margarine over very low heat, stirring constantly. Add sugar and stir until sugar is completely dissolved. Remove from heat. Continue stirring and add eggs, one at a time. Add instant pudding and walnuts until well blended. Add chocolate chips, raisins or coconut, if desired. Transfer mixture into 13″ x 9″ greased baking dish and bake 30 minutes. Brownies are ready when the top has a firm, crusty top.

Allow to cool and then slice into small squares.

Table of Promise

Throughout the seder, there are traditions that evoke the memory of being a free person. One such tradition is to recline during the meal on pillows. Another is to consume wine. Wine is a symbol of joy and certainly of being a free person.

There are many verbs used to describe how God will redeem His people. In Exodus 6:6-7, God says: 1) I will bring out, 2) I will deliver, 3) I will redeem, and 4) I will take.

Table Description

On this table of promise, the colors blue and white overshadow any other detail. These colors represent a tallit, the fringed prayer shawl of the Jewish people, and also the pattern for the flag of Israel. As we remember that Passover was about God delivering the Israelites to the Promised Land, the watery background reminds us of the Red Sea, and the lantern reminds us of our escape to freedom. The four pillar-like wine glasses filled with flowers hint at the four cups of wine ceremonially served at the Passover dinner, suggesting the ways that God protects and redeems the Israelites. You may place a small bouquet of flowers at each place setting, or simply use a colored and decorated hardboiled egg in an egg holder. To create a unique name tag, write your guest's name or initial on the egg using a metallic marker or sticker.

Shavuot

And wine that maketh glad
the heart of man.

—PSALM 104:15

Shavuot

*I am the LORD thy God,
who brought thee out of the
land of Egypt, out of the
house of bondage. Thou shalt
have no other gods before Me.*

—EXODUS 20:2

Shavuot celebrates the bounty of the spring
harvest and when the Jewish people received
the Torah from God. This gift crystallized the
relationship between God and the people of
Israel. It was the moment when the people of
Israel became a nation. The festival of Shavuot
is filled with flowers and greenery to symbolize
springtime and the birth of a people as a
nation. The food is heavy with milk and honey
to represent the life promised by God. The
table is set with baskets and seven species that
symbolize the fertility of Israel and her people.
The seven species are wheat, barley, grapes,
figs, pomegranates, olives and dates.

The gift of the Torah touched the essence of the Jewish soul for eternity. Shavuot can also be translated as "oaths," and it is the day that God swore eternal devotion to the Jewish people, while we swore everlasting loyalty to Him.

The holiday of Shavuot is a two-day holiday, beginning at sundown on the 5th of Sivan and lasting until nightfall on the 7th of Sivan. In Israel, Shavuot only lasts one day, but the rituals are the same, including women lighting candles to welcome the holiday. It is a mitzvah to stay up all night learning Torah on the first night of Shavuot, a practice called Tikkun Leil Shavuot. Dairy foods are eaten in commemoration of the people of Israel who could not cook meat in pots that had yet to be rendered kosher.

Country Living

Table Description

The setting for this Shavuot celebration is a lush country vineyard. A beautifully embroidered tablecloth sets off the burgundy, gold and earth tones of the harvest table. Baskets of bread with raw grains tucked inside, and baskets of grapes and seasonal fruit, follow a wicker theme also used for the chargers. China edged with a gold filigree pattern and a cloth napkin add to the elegant contrast between holiday finery and country charm. A snippet of grapes spilling from each napkin ring emphasizes "plenty."

...and in thee shall all the families of the earth be blessed."

—GENESIS 12:3

Shavuot is a time of plenty. Heaps of colorful produce, milk and honey flowing and a delicious assortment of wines and cheeses appeal to our senses.

Involving the Children

A mezuzah case is a wonderful gift that the children can decorate for each guest attending your Shavuot celebration, nicely representing God's gift of the Torah to the Jewish people. Plain mezuzah cases may be purchased for the children to paint and/or decorate. For an outdoor celebration, the children can make floral garlands for the guests to wear on their heads and they can also prepare decorated baskets with colorful flowers, adding dried and fresh fruit to the baskets. These make lovely gifts for the guests to take home as a reminder of the bountiful time they had with you.

Mixed Baby Greens Salad with Oranges, Cashews and Pomegranate

(Pareve) Serves 4-6

2 oranges

1 package mixed baby greens

¼ cup cashews, toasted

¼ cup pomegranate seeds

Dressing:

2 tablespoons honey

5 tablespoons olive oil

2½ tablespoons quality balsamic vinegar

3 tablespoons fresh lemon juice

2 teaspoons Dijon mustard

1 tablespoon water

Salt

For the dressing, mix all ingredients together in a small bowl until well blended. Set aside. Using a small sharp knife, peel oranges and remove white layer (pith). Working over a small bowl, cut between the membranes to release orange segments. Place greens on individual serving plates and top with orange segments, cashews and pomegranate seeds. Drizzle with dressing and serve.

Fettuccine Alfredo

(Dairy) Serves 4-6

1 pound fettuccine noodles, prepared

1 stick unsalted butter

2 garlic cloves, peeled and minced

½ pound mushrooms, sliced

1 pint heavy cream

½ cup fresh basil, chopped

1½ cups grated Parmesan cheese

Salt and white pepper

1 tablespoon mushroom powder (optional)

Basil leaves

Melt 1 tablespoon butter in sauté pan. Sauté garlic and add mushrooms, cooking until golden. Set aside. In a large saucepan, melt remaining butter and whisk in cream. Bring to a simmer and cook 15-20 minutes until very slightly thickened. Lower heat and add basil. Add mushroom mixture and cheese, stirring constantly. Season generously with white pepper and add salt to taste (and mushroom powder, if desired). Pour mixture over prepared pasta and toss gently until fully coated. Sprinkle with Parmesan cheese and garnish with basil leaves.

Ceremony of Bikkurim

And now, behold, I have brought the first of the fruit of the land, which Thou, O LORD, hast given me. And thou shalt set it down before the LORD thy God, and worship before the LORD thy God.

—DEUTERONOMY 26:10

During the time of the Temple, Shavuot marked the first day that individuals could bring the first fruits of the harvest to the Temple for the ceremony of Bikkurim, which conveyed the gratitude of the Jewish people to God for both the first fruits of the field and for His guidance throughout Jewish history. The first fruits were identified by a reed tied around the fruit as it began to ripen. These fruits were then cut down and placed in baskets made with gold and silver. The baskets were then loaded on oxen with gilded horns decorated with garlands of flowers. The procession was accompanied by music as it travelled to the Temple in Jerusalem. The ceremony at the Temple began with the reading of Deuteronomy 26:1-11, starting with God's commitment to bring us to the Promised Land (v. 1) and continuing with a reference to Jacob's time in the land of Aram: "A wandering Aramean was my father" (v. 5). The passage continues with the history of the people of Israel through their exile in Egypt, their redemption from slavery, and their subsequent return to the Land of Israel, a land flowing with milk and honey.

Table Description
Sunflower plates and centerpiece are a bright and cheerful contrast to the shiny green tablecloth and woven wicker chargers. An outdoor venue is perfect for Bikkurim, calling to remembrance the journey to the Temple with the first fruits. Garlands may be set about the table, reminiscent of the oxen and their holiday decorations.

Eggplant Roulade with Spaghetti

(Dairy) Serves 6-8

Sauce:

28-ounce can crushed tomatoes, with juice

3 tablespoons olive oil

⅓ medium onion, diced

2 garlic cloves, peeled and sliced

7 fresh basil leaves, torn in small pieces

2 tablespoons fresh oregano, chopped

¼ teaspoon sea salt

¼ teaspoon fresh ground black pepper

1 teaspoon granulated sugar

Pour tomatoes with juice into a large bowl and set aside. Heat olive oil over medium-high heat. Add onion and garlic, cooking until onion is tender and translucent. Add tomatoes, basil, oregano, salt, pepper and sugar. Bring to a boil, then reduce heat. Simmer uncovered for 30 minutes. Remove from heat and puree. Pour half of the sauce into the bottom of a 9″ x 13″ baking dish. Pour the remainder of the sauce into a large sauté pan and keep hot over medium heat.

Roulades:

2 large eggplants

Vegetable oil

¾ pound dry spaghetti

¾ cup plus 2 cups freshly grated Parmesan cheese, divided

Pinch of salt

2 cups grated mozzarella, divided

Fresh basil leaves

1 tablespoon extra-virgin olive oil

Preheat oven to 450°F. Cut eggplants lengthwise into ¼″ slices. Arrange eggplant on paper towels in single layer. Sprinkle with salt and let sit for 1 hour to eliminate excess moisture. Heat oil in large sauté pan over medium-high heat. Pat eggplant slices dry and add to oil. Cook until brown, turning once. Transfer to paper towels to absorb excess oil and allow to cool.

Cook spaghetti until just before al dente and drain. Add cooked spaghetti to sauté pan with hot tomato sauce. Add ¾ cup Parmesan and salt. Toss to mix well.

Arrange eggplant slices on a flat surface. Divide spaghetti into the number of slices of eggplant. Lay a portion of spaghetti across the width of the eggplant slice, then carefully bring the ends of the spaghetti to meet in the center of the eggplant slice. Top each portion with mozzarella and Parmesan. Roll the length of each eggplant slice around the spaghetti. Gently transfer roulade to baking dish, placing on top of sauce with the overlapping ends of the eggplant facing down. Lightly sprinkle with more mozzarella and Parmesan. Bake 10 minutes, until heated through. Garnish with basil leaves and drizzle with olive oil.

Harvest Holiday

...and the feast of harvest, the first-fruits of thy labours, which thou sowest in the field; and the feast of ingathering, at the end of the year, when thou gatherest in thy labours out of the field.

—EXODUS 23:16

In biblical times, Shavuot also marked the start of the new agricultural season and was called in Hebrew *Hag HaKatzir*, which means "the Harvest Holiday."

Table Description

In the spirit of the harvest holiday, a table is set up outdoors using colors of the soil. The table is covered in dark brown jute cloth and plates with an olive print are used to extend the outdoor feeling. Using pale brown jute, the napkins are folded in the shape of leaves and are tied with a strip of the same material. A piece of wheat is tucked into the napkin for decoration. A tall, dark reed basket-vase is the centerpiece, using wheat, rather than flowers, to represent the Counting of Omer (unit of measure) in the Temple. A wooden plate with assorted cheeses, olives and nuts is perfect for the guests to nosh on. Candles in the shape of cactus fit the environment and add candlelight to the scene. For a romantic twist to the holiday celebration, place a blanket on the grass for a Shavuot picnic. Fill a basket with raffia palm, and add a bottle of wine, some cheeses and freshly baked bread. You and your loved one can celebrate the holiday while enjoying God's creation in nature.

Candied Ginger Lemon Yogurt Cake

(Dairy) Serves 4-6

Cake:

1½ cups all-purpose flour

2 teaspoons baking powder

¼ teaspoon kosher salt

1 cup whole milk plain yogurt

1 cup sugar

3 extra large eggs

1 teaspoon lemon zest

1 teaspoon vanilla extract

½ tablespoon candied ginger, minced

½ cup vegetable oil

Syrup:

2 tablespoons water

3 tablespoons lemon juice

½ cup sugar

Glaze:

1 cup powdered sugar

2 tablespoons freshly squeezed lemon juice

Preheat oven to 350°F. Grease and flour loaf pan, tapping out excess flour.

In a medium bowl, sift together flour, baking powder and salt. In a separate bowl, whisk together yogurt, sugar, eggs, lemon zest, vanilla and ginger. Slowly add dry ingredients. Gently fold oil into batter until fully incorporated.

Pour batter into loaf pan and bake 40-50 minutes, until a cake tester comes out clean from the center.

While cake is baking, cook syrup ingredients in small saucepan until sugar is completely dissolved and syrup is clear. Set aside and allow to cool to room temperature.

When cake is done, cool in loaf pan for 10 minutes. Transfer cake to cooling rack covered with parchment paper. While cake is still warm, pour syrup over cake and allow to soak in. When cake is cool, mix together glaze ingredients in a small bowl. Transfer cake to serving platter and drizzle glaze over top.

And the LORD said
unto Moses:
"Go unto the people,
and sanctify them
to-day and to-morrow,
and let them wash
their garments."

—EXODUS 19:10

Zaman Matan Torah

And He said: "Behold, I make
a covenant; before all thy
people I will do marvels,
such as have not been wrought
in all the earth, nor in any
nation; and all the people
among which thou art shall
see the work of the LORD
that I am about to do with thee,
that it is tremendous."

—EXODUS 34:10

The Torah was given by God to the Jewish
people on Mount Sinai more than 3,300 years
ago. Jewish sages have compared this event to a
wedding between God and the Jewish people.

Table Description

*White bouquets of spring flowers joyfully line up on
the table runner surrounding tall wine-glass vases,
symbolizing our happiness and celebration of the
wedding (the moment we received the Torah).
White and gold dominate the celebration.
Luxurious white plates with gold bands duplicate
the wine glasses. Psalm books are placed on each
plate, a symbol of the gift of the Torah that we
received from God. It's time to enjoy the spring
bounty and our rich heritage.*

Milk and Honey

And He hath brought us into this place, and hath given us this land, a land flowing with milk and honey.

—DEUTERONOMY 26:9

God promised the Hebrew people a land of milk and honey, and this table honors that promise. A symbolic reason for eating dairy is that milk is the first and most sustaining food we eat as infants, and the Torah is the ultimate spiritual sustenance for the Jewish soul.

Table Description

A fun and unique setting that will excite the children at your celebration is a milk and honey table. If you have access to hay bales, use them as both the table and bench for this setting. Add a cow carafe or decanter filled with milk, and put honeycomb on yellow plates. To reduce the potential for sticky fingers, you can use honey sticks instead of honeycombs. Stuffed dates can be arranged on the plates as well, and bowls of cornflakes can be offered for the children to pour milk on and enjoy. Use bright yellow flowers for your vases to resemble bees.

Temple in Jerusalem

And thou shalt come unto the
priest that shall be in those days,
and say unto him: "I profess this
day unto the LORD thy God,
that I am come unto the land
which the LORD swore unto
our fathers to give us."

—DEUTERONOMY 26:3

The text in Deuteronomy 26:1-11 retells the
history of the Jewish people as they went into exile
in Ancient Egypt where they were enslaved and
oppressed; but God then redeemed them and
brought them to the Land of Israel. The ceremony
of Bikkurim conveys the Jews' gratitude to God, both
for the first fruits of the field and for His guidance
throughout Jewish history. The Temple in Jerusalem
was the center of worship until the first century A.D.
It was the center of sacrifices, pilgrimage and prayer.

Table Description

*A harvest buffet is a great way to incorporate the best
of seasonal flowers, produce and finger foods. Wine
goes well with cold foods, such as sandwiches. On
the buffet is a stack of square platters with a print of
houses, symbolizing our desire to re-build the Temple in
Jerusalem and again bring our first fruits to God.*

And let them make Me
a sanctuary, that I may
dwell among them.

—EXODUS 25:8

Chocolate Surprise Cheesecake

(Dairy) Serves 4-6

Crust:

1½ cups graham cracker crumbs

1 tablespoon sugar

6 tablespoons unsalted butter, melted

Filling:

1½ cups superfine sugar

2½ pounds cream cheese, softened

5 whole extra-large eggs, room temperature

2 extra-large egg yolks, room temperature

¼ cup sour cream

1 tablespoon lemon zest

1½ teaspoons pure vanilla extract

Preheat oven to 350°F. In a small bowl, combine crust ingredients until crumbs are moist. Pour crust mixture into 9″ springform pan. Press crust into bottom of pan and 1″ up the sides of pan. Bake 8 minutes and cool to room temperature.

In a medium bowl, cream together sugar and cream cheese until light and fluffy, about 5 minutes using medium-high mixer speed. Reduce mixer speed to medium and add eggs and egg yolks two at a time, mixing well. Reduce mixer speed to low and add sour cream, lemon zest and vanilla extract, mixing thoroughly. Pour into cooled crust.

Raise oven temperature to 450°F. Bake 15 minutes and then reduce oven temperature to 225°F. Bake an additional 1¼ hours. Turn off oven and open door wide. Cake will not be completely set in the center. Leave cake in open oven for 30 minutes. Transfer cake to cooling rack covered with parchment paper and let sit at room temperature until completely cooled. Wrap cake in plastic wrap and refrigerate overnight.

Ganache Glaze:

9 ounces bittersweet chocolate, chopped

1 cup heavy cream

¼ teaspoon almond extract

Ferrero Rocher candy pieces, unwrapped

Melt chocolate in a double boiler. Heat cream in a saucepan until hot, but not boiling. Stir hot cream into melted chocolate until fully incorporated. Add almond extract. Continue stirring 3 minutes, until smooth. Set aside. When cool, pour over refrigerated cake from center out. Allow excess to drip down sides of cake. Set candy pieces on top of glaze.

Then said Boaz unto Ruth:
"Hearest thou not, my daughter?
Go not to glean in another field,
neither pass from hence, but abide
here fast by my maidens."

—RUTH 2:8

Pure Elegance

Some communities read the Book of Ruth in honor of King David's passing on the 6th of Sivan, since he was a descendant of Ruth the Moabite, who followed her Israelite mother-in-law, Naomi, to live with the Jewish people. Ruth asserted the right of the poor to collect leftovers of the barley harvest, and just like Shavuot, her story takes place during the spring harvest.

Entreat me not to leave thee, and to return from following after thee; for whither thou goest, I will go; and where thou lodgest, I will lodge; thy people shall be my people, and thy God my God.

—RUTH 1:16

Table Description:

An elegant and simple table is perfect for this aspect of Shavuot. Silver, white and crystal are used with the only splash of color coming from the beautiful fruit-covered cheesecake. Use white tulips and magnolia flowers to keep the table clean and graceful. Magnolia blossoms in clear martini glasses are placed strategically around the table for the floral arrangement. Strings of imitation pearls around the table add a measure of sophistication. Crystal and silver salt and pepper shakers, designed as grape clusters hanging from the vine, match the cake plate. Beautiful silver-beaded chargers give the table another level of class, but simple silver chargers for the plates obtain the same effect.

Subtle White

And he was there with the LORD
forty days and forty nights; he did
neither eat bread, nor drink water.
And he wrote upon the tables the
words of the covenant, the ten words.

—EXODUS 34:28

Forty is the numerical value of the Hebrew word *chalav* (milk) which is equivalent to the forty days and forty nights that Moses spent on Mount Sinai before returning with the Torah, as is mentioned in the Book of Exodus. King Solomon compared the Torah to milk when he wrote, "honey and milk are under thy tongue" (Song of Songs 4:11).

Table Description

This table is a variation on the previous theme of Pure Elegance, with a special centerpiece made up of three large martini glasses, each with an open white magnolia blossom resting inside. The stately elegance of these understated arrangements complement the white china and glass chargers; their quiet dominance gives a sense of balance and harmony.

Blooming Celebration

There is a story that the Israelites found Mount Sinai blooming and lush with greenery and flowers. Even today, temples decorate the Torah scrolls with wreaths of roses in honor of this story.

Table Description

To set the table, fill a decanter with red wine, and fill flower dishes with nut and sesame clusters. For the centerpiece, use a flower-shaped pitcher in the same pink hues, and fill it with pink and white roses.

Picnic Time

Seven weeks shalt thou number unto thee; from the time the sickle is first put to the standing corn shalt thou begin to number seven weeks. And thou shalt keep the feast of weeks unto the LORD thy God...

—DEUTERONOMY 16:9-10

On Shavuot, it is tradition to enjoy delicious dairy products, such as variations of cheeses. Low fat cheeses are recommended as these are important for a healthy and nutritious diet. You can use low fat white cheeses, adding spices and fresh herbs, such as green onion or dill, and turn them into interesting and healthy dips, served with vegetables on the side. Carrots, broccoli, tomatoes and fresh grilled eggplant, or even fresh fruit, bring a sense of freshness to your palate and provide great nutritional value to your body.

Basket Description

Another option for giving homage to God's creation on this holiday is to find a beautiful garden setting or park where you can enjoy a picnic feast. Pack a white wicker basket with simple fare and don't forget to include fresh fruit, such as apples and grapes, and an apple pie for dessert. This basket has been made even more lovely by adding pink wine glasses with a gold-patterned rim, and a beautiful bouquet of flowers.

Brit Milah and Baby Naming

This is My covenant, which ye shall keep, between Me and you and thy seed after thee: every male among you shall be circumcised.

—GENESIS 17:10

The Brit Milah is also referred to by Ashkenazi Jews as a Bris. For Jewish males, it is a physical representation of the Jewish covenant with God. Newborn boys are given a Hebrew name at their Brit Milah, and that name has great spiritual significance.

There is also an opportunity for naming baby girls. The first time that the parents can be called to the bimah (pulpit) in the synagogue, a prayer is recited and the girl's Hebrew name is announced to the congregation.

Unlike a wedding where you have more time to plan for the special event, you only have eight days between the birth of your child and the Brit Milah. Here are a few suggestions that will help you with your preparations for this very special occasion. Do not hesitate to ask for help from your family and friends. Plan in advance and think of all the details that will make the ceremony and its celebration special. Select the location for the ceremony, create your guest list, contact professionals, like the mohel (a person trained in performing ritual circumcision), the photographer, and the caterer, to discuss the details of the celebration. Keep in mind that you may not be able to specify the exact day of the birth, so check whether the location that you choose has the flexibility to accommodate your event. The Brit Milah of a healthy baby is always done on the eighth day of life, even if it falls on Shabbat or a holiday. It is performed only during daylight hours, and the earlier in the day the better.

Table Description

Yellow and blue make this Brit Milah table pop. A white tablecloth reflects the sun in this breezy seaside party setting. Coordinated light blue china with white polka dots contrast with the yellow cutlery and canary yellow accents. Sunshine bright rubber ducks float on individual ponds of foil-wrapped candies as well as in the centerpiece pool of blue-tinted water topped with glitter. Sunny yellow napkins are secured with chains of baby-name beads on elastic strings. For a delightful addition, the name of the guest can be added to the rubber ducks or to a baby bottle decoration and used as place cards.

Whether it's a boy or a girl, there is no excitement like the birth of a new baby. Babies can decide to appear early or late, so if possible, be sure to schedule your joyful celebration well before the due date.

Involving the Children

Give each guest a 5″ x 5″ square of fabric and special markers so they can decorate the square and add their own blessing for the newborn. After collecting all the squares, you can make them into a keepsake quilt for the baby. You may also ask the children to help decorate a basket that can be used as a centerpiece for the table, to be filled with small stuffed animals. After the ceremony, the centerpiece and its contents can be given to children in need. Use this opportunity to explain to the children the concept of Tikkun Olam (Repairing the World).

Greek Salad

(Dairy) Serves 4-6

4 cucumbers, seeds removed and sliced into ¼" moons

4 tomatoes, diced

½ cup Kalamata olives, pitted

I cup feta cheese, crumbled

I red bell pepper, seeds removed and cut into I" pieces

½ small red onion, sliced

I head Romaine lettuce, chopped or shredded (optional)

Dressing:

½ cup olive oil

¼ cup fresh squeezed lemon juice

I teaspoon dried oregano

I tablespoon fresh parsley, chopped

Salt and pepper to taste

Toss all ingredients together in a bowl with dressing and serve.

Teal & White Symphony

And God blessed them; and God said unto them: "Be fruitful, and multiply, and replenish the earth, and subdue it; and have dominion over the fish of the sea, and over the fowl of the air, and over every living thing that creepeth upon the earth."

—GENESIS 1:28

"Blessed be his arrival" (*Baruch HaBa*) is the traditional greeting at a ritual circumcision. Just as parents "give away" their children at the wedding, or the Torah is passed from one generation to another at the Bar or Bat Mitzvah, the infant is passed from parent to God-parent to the sandek. The sandek is an honored guest who holds the child during the ritual circumcision. To participate in the performance of a commandment (mitzvah), especially one that binds a boy to the covenant, is a high honor. Jewish tradition holds that one should be eager to fulfill a mitzvah, so the Brit Milah is best done at first light in a synagogue or home.

Table Description

A white tablecloth with a chiffon circle overlay is set with gold chargers to show off pale blue china with a butterfly detail. Blue mother of pearl handled flatware sparkles and reflects the blue in the small glass balls in the vase that makes the centerpiece. Pale blue dyed ostrich feathers add a sense of whimsy to the table, while cobalt blue glasses add a grounded element.

Spinach, Swiss Chard and Kale Lasagna

(Dairy) Serves 4-6

1 package lasagna noodles, prepared

2 tablespoons olive oil

4 garlic cloves, peeled and minced

4 shallots, peeled and minced

2 cups washed spinach, cut in ½" pieces

2 cups washed Swiss chard, cut in ½" pieces

2 cups washed kale, cut in ½" pieces

2 tablespoons sun-dried tomatoes, diced

4 cups mozzarella cheese, shredded

2 cups grated Parmesan cheese

Béchamel sauce:

1 stick butter

¾ cup flour

2½ cups milk

1 pinch nutmeg

Melt butter in a large high-sided sauté pan. When butter is melted, stir in flour ¼ cup at a time until fully incorporated, 2-3 minutes. Heat milk in a saucepan until hot, but not boiling. Slowly add hot milk to flour mixture, stirring constantly. When milk is completely absorbed by flour and a thick, smooth sauce is created, add nutmeg. Turn heat to low, stirring occasionally until ready to use.

Preheat oven to 350°F. Prepare lasagna noodles according to the package directions and drain.

In a separate sauté pan, heat olive oil and add garlic and shallots, cooking until golden brown. Add spinach, Swiss chard and kale, and allow to cook down. Drain excess liquid, and add sun-dried tomatoes.

In a 9" x 13" greased baking dish, make layers of lasagna noodles, greens mixture, mozzarella, Parmesan, and Béchamel sauce. Repeat layers until the dish is full, finishing with a layer of Béchamel and Parmesan cheese. Bake 30-45 minutes or until top is golden brown and cheese has melted.

Naming a Princess

Lo, children are a heritage of the LORD,
the fruit of the womb is a reward.

—PSALM 127:3

Table Description

A white tablecloth with a chiffon circle overlay is set with square pink floral plates and floral bowls. Bowls are filled with pink and red feathers and plastic eggs are personalized with your guests' names using stick-on letters. Pink water glasses with gold accents echo the shades of pink in the plates. Red robins in their nests perch cheerfully on the wreath centerpiece. Red roses may also be used on the wreath centerpiece to welcome your daughter as a Rose of Israel.

Sole with Mushroom or Lemon Sauce

(Dairy) Serves 4-6

6 fillets of sole, boneless and skinless

¼ cup fresh lemon juice

2 eggs

3 tablespoons heavy cream

Salt and pepper

1 cup all-purpose flour

¼ cup canola oil

Pre-heat oven to 200°F. Arrange fillets in baking dish. Pour lemon juice over fish and let sit for 5 minutes. Season fish with salt and pepper on both sides. Beat eggs with cream until smooth. Lightly cover fish first in flour, then egg mixture. Heat oil in large pan and add fish, frying until golden, about 2-3 minutes on each side. Remove from pan, blotting with paper towels to absorb excess oil. Arrange fillets in a clean baking dish and keep warm in oven.

Mushroom Sauce:

4 tablespoons unsalted butter, divided

12 ounces white mushrooms, sliced

½ cup heavy cream

½ cup shallots, peeled and minced

1 tablespoon all-purpose flour

1¾ cup white wine

Salt and pepper

2 tablespoons parsley, chopped

In a large high-sided sauté pan, melt 2 tablespoons butter. Add mushrooms and cook until golden brown. Drain mushrooms, reserving liquid, and set aside. In a small saucepan over low-medium heat, warm heavy cream, but do not bring to boil. Melt remaining butter in sauté pan. Add shallots and cook until translucent. Whisk flour into sauté pan and cook 2-3 minutes, stirring constantly. Add wine and liquid from mushrooms, stirring constantly until incorporated. Simmer until sauce thickens. Slowly add heavy cream, stirring constantly. Add mushrooms and simmer until heated through. Add salt and pepper to taste. Pour mushroom sauce over fillets and sprinkle with parsley.

Lemon Sauce:

2 tablespoons butter

4 garlic cloves, peeled and minced

⅔ cup lemon juice

Parsley or dill, finely chopped

½ cup almonds, toasted

Melt butter in a medium sauté pan. Add garlic, cooking until translucent. Add lemon juice, stir, and turn off heat. Pour lemon sauce over fillets and sprinkle fillets with parsley or dill and almonds.

And Leah said: "God hath endowed me with a good dowry; now will my husband dwell with me, because I have borne him six sons." And she called his name Zebulun. And afterwards she bore a daughter, and called her name Dinah.

—GENESIS 30:20-21

Thank Heaven for Baby Girls

In the modern, more egalitarian western world, you will find a parallel celebration of Brit Milah for girls. The counterweight traditional view is that the domain of women was private and the domain of men was public, which precluded a public celebration of a female. Through a process of creativity, connecting what is understood about our tradition and the needs of a community, Judaism adapts. The notion of Simchat Bat (celebrating a daughter) or Bat Brit (daughter of the covenant) has come into vogue. Usually during a Shabbat service, parents are called to the bimah (pulpit) where they receive honor as a part of the service, and the daughter is then given her Hebrew name. The celebratory meal after services is typically sponsored, at least in part, by the family of the newborn daughter.

Table Description

A fuchsia satin tablecloth is the start of this celebratory table. Each place setting is delightfully inviting. Ruffled pink chargers are topped with butterfly-shaped salad plates. The centerpiece is a tall, feminine, boot-shaped vase filled with pink and white marshmallows and topped with heart-shaped lollypops. Opaque pink wine glasses hold small pink baby bottles filled with an instant fudge mix for your guests to take home. The wine glasses sport a happy cupcake print. Miniature baby rattles and hearts in pink are scattered all over to complement the look of the table.

Tiramisu

(Dairy) Serves 4-6

¾ cup coffee liqueur

¾ cup water

4 tablespoons instant espresso

8 tablespoons powdered sugar, divided

16 ounces mascarpone cheese

1 cup heavy cream

1 small bar of dark chocolate

2 packages ladyfingers

4 teaspoons ground chocolate

In a glass measuring cup, whisk together coffee liqueur, water, instant espresso, and 4 tablespoons powdered sugar until smooth. Set aside ½ cup of this mixture.

Using a hand mixer, beat the remaining coffee mixture and remaining powdered sugar into the mascarpone cheese until just smooth. Do not over beat or the texture of the mascarpone will become gritty. Set aside. Whip the heavy cream until soft peaks form. Gently fold the whipped cream into the mascarpone mixture. Melt chocolate in a double boiler.

Quickly dip each side of ladyfingers in the coffee mixture; do not leave in the mixture for any length of time or the ladyfingers will become very soggy. Place a layer of ladyfingers in the bottom of an 8″ x 8″ baking dish, and spoon a layer of the mascarpone mixture over them, spreading gently to cover the ladyfingers. You may also make 4-6 individual servings in small dessert dishes. Drop a spoonful of melted chocolate over the layer of mascarpone and then repeat the layering with ladyfingers, mascarpone and melted chocolate. Add a final layer of ladyfingers and mascarpone mixture and then sprinkle with ground chocolate. Cover with plastic wrap and refrigerate for at least 90 minutes before serving.

Royal Peacock

The LORD bless thee and keep thee; the LORD make His face to shine upon thee, and be gracious unto thee; the LORD lift up His countenance upon thee, and give thee peace.

—NUMBERS 6:24-26

The ritual circumcision is a very short procedure lasting ten to fifteen minutes. The events before and after the actual operation are what calls for the help of friends and family. It will be an honor for your loved ones to help you. It is important for you to understand the after-care needs of your newborn son by following the instructions of the mohel because the infant now has a wound that needs proper care.

Table Description

An aqua blue satin tablecloth is the anchor for this table decorated in shades of blues and greens. Chargers are covered with peacock feathers and topped with white plates and white napkins fitted with peacock napkin rings. Iridescent blue-green goblets match the large vase used for the centerpiece. The vase is filled with peacock feathers and draped with plastic beaded necklaces in shades of blue.

Coconut Cake with Chocolate Ganache Filling

(Dairy) Serves 6-8

3 sticks unsalted butter

2 cups granulated sugar

5 large eggs at room temperature

1½ teaspoons vanilla extract

3 cups self-rising flour

1 teaspoon kosher salt

½ cup milk

¾ cup coconut milk

8 ounces plus 6 ounces dried
  sweetened coconut, shredded

Chocolate Ganache Filling:

1 pound dark chocolate,
  chopped in small pieces

2 cups heavy cream

Frosting:

1 pound cream cheese at
  room temperature

2 sticks unsalted butter, softened

¾ teaspoon vanilla extract

¼ teaspoon coconut extract

1 pound powdered sugar, sifted

Chocolate Ganache Filling:

Melt dark chocolate in a double boiler. Heat cream in a saucepan until hot, but not boiling. Stir hot cream into melted chocolate until fully incorporated. Continue stirring 3 minutes. Put chocolate ganache into refrigerator to thicken, which will take some time.

Frosting:

Beat together cream cheese and butter until well combined and fluffy. Add extracts and continue to beat until flavors are incorporated. Gradually add powdered sugar until spreading consistency is attained.

Cake:

Preheat oven to 350°F. Grease two 9″ round cake pans and lightly flour to prevent sticking. Tap out excess flour and set aside.

With an electric mixer, cream together butter and sugar until light yellow and fluffy. Using mixer on medium speed, add eggs one at a time. Add vanilla extract and mix well, scraping sides of bowl frequently.

In a separate bowl, sift together flour and salt. Using mixer at low speed, add to batter one-third at a time flour, milk and coconut milk. Mix until just combined. Using a spatula, fold in ½ cup coconut.

Pour batter evenly into the 2 cake pans and smooth the tops with a knife. Place pans in the center of oven and bake 45-55 minutes, or until the tops of cakes are brown and a cake tester comes out clean from the center. Place pans on cooling rack for 30 minutes. Remove cakes from pans and place on racks to finish cooling.

Carefully spread the chilled ganache over the bottom layer of cake, and place second layer on top of first. Spread frosting over top and sides of assembled cake. Sprinkle with remaining coconut, pressing to settle coconut into frosting.

It's a Boy!

Table Description

A silver-blue tablecloth sets the base of this table. Silver chargers are topped with bright white and light blue glass plates. Light blue patterned napkins are fanned out and secured by silver napkin rings. The muted pink vase centerpiece highlights the hydrangeas. White wine glasses are a brilliant contrast to the iridescent tones of the tablecloth. Miniature bags proclaiming "It's a Boy" complete the table's look, along with the blue and white glass stones scattered about the table.

Buffet Style

Welcome Baby Cupcakes

For added enjoyment, you may wish to include cupcakes, which are very popular. Many specialty shops offer customization and they can be created with great detail.

Assortment of Fruits

Another great decoration for the buffet at your Brit Milah is a homemade arrangement of fruit. Put different fruit pieces on skewers and then stick all the skewers into a green Styrofoam ball. If you don't have access to Styrofoam balls, use a foil-wrapped orange or grapefruit as your base. Make sure the entire shape is filled with fruit. This effect can also be created with vegetables using broccoli, cauliflower, cherry tomatoes, carrots and olives.

THIS BASKET OF *TOYS* IS BEING⁀G DONATED FOR
CHILDREN IN NEED BY THE MO⁀ORRIS FAMILY

Baby Boy Celebration

Use a flower arrangement for your centerpiece, or take the opportunity to create a centerpiece that can serve a dual purpose. Use a collection of small toys, arranged in a basket, to donate to a charity that supports children. This could be a beautiful gift from your newborn child. It is never too early to teach your child about caring for others, and Tzedakah (Charity/Justice).

Hosting Tips

It is important to leave room on the table for all the serving dishes, plates and glasses. Plan your table arrangement carefully so it is viewed as clean and organized, and not overly busy. Make sure the centerpiece with flowers and candles are low to the table so there is not a feeling that the centerpiece needs to be moved before the meal in order to have room for the serving dishes, or to enjoy unobstructed conversation.

Baby Bear Bread

Delight your guests with this bear-shaped loaf of bread. Let your creativity bloom!

Small Things Make a Difference

You can put your creativity in high gear when designing party favors and place cards for a Brit Milah. Rattles, ornamental diaper pins, lollipops with baby faces and, of course, baby bottles provide lots of opportunity to achieve a fun, personalized look. Be sure to pick two or three theme colors and go for it.

Hosting Tips

This is your son's first introduction to your family and friends. If you want your son to wear a special outfit for his Brit Milah, be sure to order it in advance. You should also buy a matching soft blanket to wrap him in when you give him to the mohel for the ceremony. An excellent way to celebrate the occasion is to create a photo collage that includes pictures following your family from the birth through the Brit Milah. A picture of the newborn can be printed on lollipops or chocolates. Another option is to print the birth announcement on a chocolate bar wrapper and give them out at the Brit Milah.

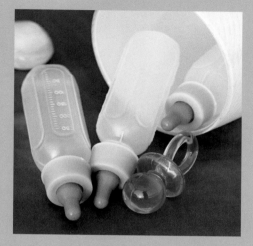

Parties

Parties

Parties should be thrown with love and joy, and proper planning can make impressive events easy to host.

Add a sense of fun to a birthday dinner with a unique cup cake. Invitations can hint at the theme, and you can encourage that presents be theme-based. For a more personalized touch, you can include a photograph of the guest of honor in the invitation, along with a map and photo of the venue or home.

If you are doing the cooking yourself, shop at bulk stores to save money. If hiring a caterer, arrange a tasting prior to the event to be certain that the food will please your guests.

Menu options are limitless, from appetizers only to a dessert buffet and everything in between. While good wine and champagne are always crowd pleasers, a few signature cocktails can impress and reduce the amount of alchohol purchased. Having a few non-alcoholic options available lets your guests who do not drink know that they have not been forgotten.

Finally, remember that a great host mingles with all of their guests!

Involving the Children

When it's time to prepare for the party, ask the children what each one can do; after all, it's easier and more fun when you have an excited team to help you. They can personalize each guest's wine glass by writing their names on them.

Mother's Day

Motherhood: All love begins and ends there.

—ROBERT BROWNING

The power of creation, growth, love, and sacrifice is embodied in one word: mother. Laughably, the day that is set aside for mothers is only 24 hours. Whether it was 3:00 a.m. or 3:00 p.m., 365 days a year, a mother's work is NEVER done. Our Jewish matriarchs in the Torah—Sarah, Rebekah, Rachel and Leah—are the women we hope our daughters emulate. The Jewish Bible is full of other mothers who are also extraordinary. Reading through the pages we find Hanna, the mother of prayer, in the Book of Samuel. In the Book of Ruth, we find the grandmother of King David who turned her life upside down to take care of her mother-in-law, Naomi. In the Book of Genesis, the mother of all humans, Eve, provides the uniquely feminine strength to overcome child birth, child rearing, and creating family love and tradition. Mother's Day is a celebration of every mom who has been the battery to charge the lives of humanity's future. Making her day special can be an act of honor, love, reflection and awareness.

Table Description

This elegant table is designed in colors of cream and pink glow. A lovely pink tablecloth holds white chargers that are decorated with pearl beads. These are topped with classic white plates. On each plate is a small swan-shaped vase that carries pink roses, blending into the centerpiece, a larger vase in the shape of a mother swan with two chicks swimming nearby. The mother swan holds a bouquet of flowers in pinks, whites and greens. Pink wine glasses decorated in gold, and napkins embraced by pearl napkin rings, complete the charming style of this table.

Summer Rolls

(Pareve) Serves 4-6

12 rice paper roll wrappers

2-3 carrots, cut into julienne strips

1 small cucumber, peeled, halved, seeded
and cut into julienne strips

3 scallions, trimmed and cut into julienne strips

1 cup bean sprouts

½ cup shredded purple cabbage

1 head of lettuce, leaves separated, washed
and ribs removed

½ pound firm tofu, cut into strips

1 bunch fresh mint, chopped

1 bunch cilantro leaves, chopped

Peanut Sauce:

1 cup coconut milk

½ cup water

½ cup creamy peanut butter

1 tablespoon sweet chili sauce

1 tablespoon soy sauce

2 teaspoons fresh lemon juice

Mix vegetables together, carrots through cabbage.

Prepare rice paper according to package directions. Place lettuce leaves on one rice paper at a time, laying the leaf on the edge closest to you and leaving 1″ of rice paper exposed at the opposite end. Place a portion of mixed vegetables, a tofu strip, mint and cilantro on top of each lettuce leaf. Fold the nearest edge of the rice paper over the filling, tuck in the sides and roll tightly to the edge on the far side. Place filled roll on a plate and cover with plastic wrap.

In a heavy bottomed saucepan, combine all ingredients for peanut sauce over low heat and bring to a boil. Remove saucepan from heat, bringing peanut sauce to room temperature. Sauce will thicken as it cools. Serve with summer rolls.

Silver Anniversary

Therefore shall a man leave his father and his mother, and shall cleave unto his wife, and they shall be one flesh.

—GENESIS 2:24

The celebration of 25 years of marriage is a major accomplishment in our time. It speaks of a couple who has travelled together despite the forks in the road, different destinations and passions that affect each person. Without a doubt, marriage builds stability in our society because it demands that we shift our attention from selfishness to giving. A marriage that lasts 25 years and continues to grow has absorbed the Jewish value, chesed—kindness. Chesed is more than just being polite or nice; it means to go beyond yourself and to extend yourself to help another, especially a beloved spouse. Preparing a silver anniversary party is a unique opportunity to help a loved one celebrate their life in conjunction with their loved one. Helping to celebrate any anniversary is a way to honor the couple and the strength of matrimony.

Table Description

A gorgeous Battenberg lace tablecloth is the anchor for this beautiful table. A silver embroidered runner is placed in the center of the table and is topped by a silver candelabra with silver candles to bring the look to eye level. A second candleholder cushions a pillar candle wrapped in silver beads and is surrounded by white votive candles. Mirrored chargers at each place setting reflect the candlelight as well as the elegant silver and crystal adornments. This is, indeed, the occasion to bring out the good china that typically gathers dust in your hutch throughout the year!

Spicy Orange Beef
(Meat) Serves 4-6

5 tablespoons soy sauce

3 tablespoons cornstarch

1½ pounds flank steak or skirt steak, cut in thin strips on the bias

4 tablespoons canola oil

2 tablespoons ginger, minced

Sauce:

3 tablespoons dry sherry

2 tablespoons Hoisin sauce

2 tablespoons honey

2 tablespoons chili sauce

3 tablespoons soy sauce

1 cup orange juice, fresh squeezed

Garnish:

5 scallions chopped

½ teaspoon orange zest

½ teaspoon lemon zest

3 tablespoons toasted sesame seeds

Baby corn

Pansy blossoms

Prepare marinade by combining soy sauce and cornstarch in a large container. Toss beef in marinade until fully coated. Cover and marinate 25 minutes in refrigerator. Whisk together sauce ingredients until completely combined. Drain and discard marinade from beef. In a large pan or wok, heat oil on high. Add beef and ginger. Cook for 3 minutes. Add sauce and cook another 5 minutes on medium heat until sauce thickens. Serve on a warm platter of rice, garnished with scallions, orange and lemon zest and sesame seeds. Add baby corn and pansy blossoms for an eye-pleasing contrast.

Banana Fritters with Maple Syrup

(Pareve) Serves 4-6

1 cup self-rising flour

¼ teaspoon baking powder

4 tablespoons sugar

2 teaspoons vanilla extract

¼ cup club soda

1 large egg

½ teaspoon salt

1 tablespoon rum

6 bananas, peeled and cut into round slices, about ½″ (or your choice)

3 tablespoons canola oil

Maple syrup, good quality

1 cup chocolate, melted

¼ cup superfine sugar

Seasonal berries

Combine flour and baking powder in a medium bowl. Set aside. In a separate bowl, mix remaining ingredients, sugar through rum, until batter is smooth. Dip banana slices into flour first and then batter until well coated. Heat oil in large sauté pan over medium-high heat. Add fritters until golden. Transfer fritters to paper towels to remove excess oil. Drizzle with maple syrup, melted chocolate or sugar and top with berries.

Guys' Night In

In my house I'm the boss, my wife is just the decision maker.

—WOODY ALLEN

Why should women have all the fun? Throw a Guys' Night In party!

Table Description

Set the table with black bandana fabric, adding black chargers with silver plates. Fashion black ribbons to look like bow ties around folded white napkins. Dishes filled with mixed nuts should be scattered throughout the room, and don't forget the crystal ashtray filled with cigars on the table. For the birthday boy, place a mug at his seat that proclaims he is the boss. Dishes with dice and poker chips can also be placed on the table. Black crystal votive candleholders make up the centerpiece. And to state the obvious, the menu should include buffalo chicken wings.

Animal Lovers

A good plan considers events before, during and after the event. Imagine the possibilities if you ask yourself, "How can I impress my guests the moment they arrive?" Or, "How can I make the centerpiece of the table strongly deliver the message of joy, elegance, and celebration?" Finally, consider making changes to the environment; for instance, add candlelight or a disco globe to change lighting. Even streamers can change the mood of a room from utilitarian and pretty to party central.

Table Description

Imagine Noah and his family on the ark celebrating God's creation. Use carved wooden napkin rings that represent the animals Noah took with him on the ark: giraffes, frogs, zebras and snakes! The centerpiece is a square vase filled with shimmering azure water (blue food coloring) reminding us of the flood, and dazzling bright orange flowers that reveal the beauty of God's creation as the waters receded. The striking colors fit in with the color pallet scheme: orange, green and blue hues giving a pleasant, exciting and cheerful ambiance.

Cake Ice Cream Cones

(Pareve) Serves 4-6

1 box of your favorite cake mix

1 teaspoon vanilla extract

16 ounces dark chocolate, chopped

24 flat-bottomed ice cream cones

Sprinkles, assorted nuts, candies

Preheat oven to 350°F. Prepare cake according to box instructions, adding vanilla extract. Place ice cream cones in muffin tins or on cookie sheet and fill each half full with batter. Bake 20 minutes or until cake springs back to the touch. Set aside to cool. Melt chocolate in a double boiler. When cool, dip tops of cones with cake into melted chocolate. Roll cake in sprinkles, nuts or candies for decoration.

Fashionistas

Women are always beautiful.

—VILLE VALO

Fashion's Night Out is a big deal in cities like New York and Los Angeles. Take that energy and throw a fashionista party.

Table Description

Small wire dress frames can be decorated with fabric to create one-of-a-kind fashion for the centerpiece. A white-on-white embroidered tablecloth creates the runway for your party. Plum colored napkins add a pop of color while brown glazed terracotta chargers ground your collection. Place costume jewelry all around the table and on the dress forms. Place a party favor bracelet in each coffee cup. Dessert is a four-piece Chocolate Ballotine Box wrapped in designer paper. You and your guests can watch videos of New York Fashion Week to complete the experience. The items on the table are meant to be takeaway gifts. You can make a game of it by having your guests draw numbers to take home their pick.

The Cheshire Cat's Tea Party

People are pet crazy. Show that you know about your friends' love of cats with this goofy cat tea party.

Table Description

The table is covered with a tablecloth made of faux fur and the plates are a fun, cat-themed set. After the party, these can be given to the guest of honor. Little balls of yarn are scattered all over the table and two cat-shaped teapots snuggle down in the center of the table. One pot can be filled with traditional tea and the other can hold an herbal tea for those who don't drink caffeine. Small glass fish bowls can be filled with black and white candies with a tea candle placed in the center for additional decoration. As a party favor, a candy mouse can be placed in each tea cup before the party starts. If candy mice aren't easily accessible, a cat toy can be placed in the tea cup instead.

Bow Wow Wow!

Games have rules, helping to make your guests comfortable because they will know what is expected of them. Some of your guests may not feel as comfortable as others in social situations, so game playing adds a dimension of security and fun. Googling "party games" will give you thousands of options! Take a chance, let yourself become a bit silly and your guests will all let down their guard and begin to party with you.

Table Description

This adorable buffet setting will delight all of your guests, especially the pet lovers. The table is covered with a red faux fur tablecloth, and is set buffet-style with fun dog-themed plates. These can be given to the birthday guest after the party. A paw print mug makes a grrrrreat holder for the silverware. Fill a dog-shaped cookie jar with chocolate-dipped marshmallows for a tasty dessert. Place new dog toys on the table as decorations and use new funny dog collars to hold the napkins.

Bark If You Love Polka Dots!

Table Description

The pet lovers theme continues with a cheery red and white polka dot tablecloth setting off white chargers with black rimmed plates (and more polka dots) printed with Scottish Terriers. Black napkins with, you guessed it—white polka dots, beautifully complement the tablecloth and plates. Spot and Sparky make cute centerpieces, using Sparky's lower half to hold popcorn. Popcorn is also available in red mugs for the guests to nibble on. Tall red glasses, with new dog collars wrapped around, hold other yummy treats and can be taken home as party favors.

Index